Backpacking

"Beginner or expert will find this volume a real time-saver in preparing and an irreplaceable companion on the trail."—*San Francisco Examiner-Chronicle*

"This carefully written how-to-do-it book is an excellent introduction to the outdoors for beginners . . . making this a fine buyer's guide for newly converted lovers of the outdoors."—*The Real Paper*

"Comprehensive, extremely useful. A light tone, leeway for idiosyncratic personal choices, and just enough detail should assure a popular following."—*Kirkus Reviews*

Backpacking

A COMPLETE GUIDE TO WH

LEE SCHREIBER

evised and Updated

OW, AND WHERE FOR HIKERS AND BACKPACKERS

d the Editors of Backpacking Journal

A SCARBOROUGH BOOK
SB STEIN AND DAY/*Publishers*/New York

To
J, K, M and M (again)
&
Stan and Dolly Kleckner

REVISED SCARBOROUGH BOOKS EDITION 1983

Copyright © 1978 by Davis Publications, Inc.,
Copyright © 1983 by Lee Schreiber
All rights reserved, Stein and Day, Incorporated
Designed by Irene Friedman
Printed in the United States of America
Stein and Day / *Publishers*
Scarborough House
Briarcliff Manor, N.Y. 10510

Library of Congress Cataloging in Publication Data

Schreiber, Lee.
  Backpacking: a complete guide to why, how, and
where for hikers and backpackers.

  1. Backpacking. 2. Backpacking—United States.
I. Backpacking journal. II. Title.
GV199.6.S35 1983   796.5′1   82-42860
ISBN 0-8128-6187-6 (pbk)

If a label is required, say that I am one who loves unfenced country.

—Edward Abbey

Acknowledgments

CONTRIBUTORS:
Louis V. Bignami
Andrew J. Carra
Sam Curtis
Marlyn S. Doan
Dave Engerbretson
Don Geary
Martin Hanft
Jorma Hyypia
Michele S. Kay
Charles Self
Bill Thomas
Jim Dale Vickery

TITLE PAGE PHOTOGRAPH:
Mark J. Boesch

Contents

Section I

Section II

"Walking-Tent," Under-the-Pack, Over-the-Pack; Narrow Poncho—Jackets, Rain Pants, Cagoule, Testing Rain Gear, Keeping Feet Dry); Keeping Gear Dry

Section III

Detour Impassable Promontories, Hike Wide Beaches, Eat Properly, Keep Dry); Good Coastlines (Point Reyes, Calif., National Seashore, Cape Hatteras, N.C., National Seashore, Olympic, Wash., National Park, Oregon Dunes National Recreation Area); Climate Protection from the Sun; Fresh Water, Insects

Major Manufacturers of Backpacking Equipment and Related Gear

Introduction

If you are a follower of subtitles, do not be too far misled down a garden path. A COMPLETE GUIDE TO WHY, HOW AND WHERE FOR HIKERS AND BACKPACKERS. That *should* cover most of it. Indeed, this book is a complete guide—though, admittedly, far from *compleat*. And it certainly has its fair allotment of Hows and Wheres; you can look it up. But I, too, wonder, as another potential pathfinder, *where* is Why?

Where is the chapter on the "Psychology of the Solitary Backpacker." depicting and delineating his/her psychic trails and travails? It's not here. Nor is there a chapter containing pertinent quotes from notorious outdoorpersons. For example: "In wilderness is the preservation of the world." A major conservation group uses that as its slogan but fails to credit the sloganeer—Henry David Thoreau.

We could have done an entire chapter on Mr. Thoreau's oft-quoted and least-cited lines. That would have accounted for *his* version of Why. But we had spatial considerations; there was no more room. There was some talk about bumping off one of the other pertinent, albeit dry, sections; Orienting Compass and Map was in definite jeopardy. In the end, we eschewed Quotation Without

Declination and decided to go with a short, breezy introduction to explain it all away.

We realize that backpacking is a serious business (see Manufacturers' List), but it is not *solemn*. Backpacking is for physical conditioning, for practicing self-reliance, for learning skills, for going from Point A to Point B, for getting away from people, for meeting people, for seeing new places, for buying needless equipment, for sleeping under the stars, for traveling cheaply, for communing with wildlife, for taking pictures/leaving footprints, for preserving natural beauty. But it's also fun. *That's* why.

—L. S.

Section I

1 Packs and Frames

With over 400 different packs available from several dozen separate manufacturers it's not surprising that the correct choice is difficult. What is surprising is that you see so few people on the trail with packs that are properly fitted to their body and needs. It seems that everybody had gone into the shop and picked the largest and most expensive pack they could find.

Your first step should be to determine whether you really need a day pack, weekend pack or an expeditionary pack. For most of us a weekend pack is sufficient for all our trips save the one biggie each year when we could really *rent* a larger pack. This is a very useful option for limited use gear, and most shops offer big frame packs for about $5 a day. That's a small investment if it will let you tote less for the rest of the year. You probably should consider a weekend-size pack for your basic model.

This type of pack holds between 1,500 and 2,500 cubic inches and is more than adequate for three or four days. You can get a rough idea of the size you need by bundling together all your backpacking gear on the floor. You can also tote your gear down to the shop for an on-the-spot fitting.

The real limiting factor to this class of pack is weight rather than cubic capacity. If your loads average about 35 pounds, you should think about a frame and pack combination. If your loads for *weekends* average above 35 pounds you should think of having an equipment sale; you're chugging up the trail with entirely too much gear. Compulsive photographers and fishermen are excepted, of course; we really *do* need two rods and six lenses.

If your gear and food weighs in at less than the 35-pound figure, you should head for the nearest mountain shop or send away for catalogs. A large mountain shop will provide you with the best possible combination of skilled help and wide selection. Discount houses and chain drugstores just don't have the expertise to fit you with the proper gear, and unless you know exactly what you want, avoid them.

If you're too shy or your gear too tacky to lug to the shop, you might take three or four gallon milk containers to the shop. Fill with the amount of water that approximates your normal load. All adjustments should be made with a loaded pack, while you're wearing about what you would wear on the trail. Even minute differences in adjustment can mean a lot in the way a pack feels under load; emulating field conditions is vital for the best results.

These internal frame packs are from Himalayan. The Avalanche (left) holds 2,280 cubic inches and weighs three pounds, eight ounces; it sells for $92. The Summit (right) contains 1,194 cubic inches and weighs four pounds; this convertible pack sells for $40.

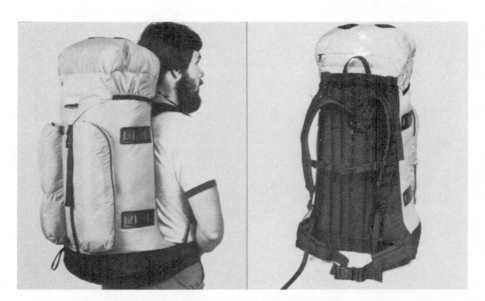

The MonoLITE from Alpenlite is another internal frame pack. It holds a capacious 4,000 cubic inches and weighs one pound, 15½ ounces. Suggested retail price: $100.

The initial sizing of packs takes into consideration the distance between the hip belt attachment and the shoulder. You want the belt to be tight without constricting, and the shoulder height should be such that you can move your shoulders without moving the loaded pack.

The importance of a correctly fitting hip belt cannot be overemphasized, unless you're one of the hipless types that can't keep one up. The hip belt is the base of your load carrying system, and it puts the weight on your hips and legs instead of your shoulders and arms. You should be aware that while many packs come with hip belts you can also add different belts more suited to you. Belts aren't very expensive and are an easy way to upgrade your present equipment. Just be sure your belt has some kind of quick-release buckle; so if you happen to fall off a log into a stream, you'll be able to get out of your pack.

Once the belt is adjusted, you can start adjusting the other areas. The shoulder width is critical: too wide and the pack will come off your shoulder; too narrow and you'll feel as if Bigfoot is squeezing your neck. On some packs you can adjust the angle that the straps come off the pack; this can be a key factor in comfortable toting.

Load-lifter straps running from the top of your shoulder to the upper part of the pack are worthwhile features on many designs. These straps help keep the pack high and tight to your body for the most comfortable fit. They also allow you to adjust your pack so you can take the weight off your hips and put it on your shoulders for short stretches.

The width of the shoulder straps is critical, too. Wide straps distribute weight more evenly. However, narrow straps on an otherwise excellent pack can easily be remedied with the addition of foam pads.

On both packs and pack bags for frames you'll find a huge number of different designs and internal division systems. In weekend packs internal divisions aren't really critical. Most packs offer top and bottom sections for your gear. The bigger frame packs usually have more divisions, which is a good way to keep the item you want from migrating to the bottom of a big, undivided sack. If you do buy a horizontally divided pack, be sure to check that there's

The Winans' Camel from Cannondale weighs six pounds, two ounces and holds 4,300 cubic inches. Its frame is a single tube of 7/8-inch aluminum alloy. The pack bag is made of Cordura nylon. It's adjustable to fit anyone from five feet to 6 feet, 8 inches tall. The Camel sells for about $150.

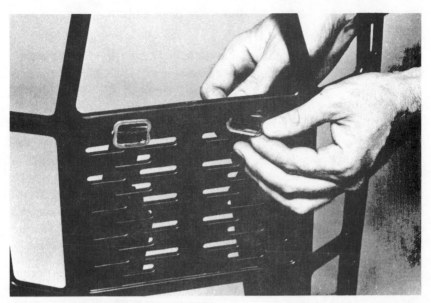

Quick adjustment on Peak 1™ frames is by means of Lash-Tabs™. These are metal tabs on the ends of straps that slip through any slot in the frame, twist, and the pack is attached securely. Every fitting adjustment can be made without tools. When traveling by plane, car, train or thumb, the straps and belts can be removed and stuffed inside the pack. *(Coleman Company)*

either a zipper or partial floor arangement so that tent poles, fishing rod cases and other long items can be inserted down the side of the pack.

Lots of lash points are very handy, as are a good selection of pockets. Most packs feature a flap map pocket, side pockets—sometimes double—and a large back pocket. If you're also going to use your pack for ski touring, make sure the pockets don't interfere with your arm swing.

Moving to the specifics of pack shape and design, we find a dismayingly large number of options. None are really bad if the pack comes from a reputable source, and most have one or more uses for which they are ideally suited. The choice then becomes one of finding a designer who uses his pack the way you do.

Design types include monocoque, internal X-stay, H-stay, Y-frame, perimeter frame and convertible frameless packs that you can add to a frame for carrying heavier weights. There are also traditional European rucksacks available. These are popular with climbers and cross-country skiers who appreciate the maximum flexibility and freedom of movement of the frameless pack and are willing to limit themselves to light loads.

For weekend packs the monocoque is increasingly the experts' choice. It can work for you if you consistently carry the same amount of gear and practice stuffing your pack tight. This is particularly important in the bottom section. In this design the tightly-packed contents provide the frame effect; you save some weight and get a superbly comfortable weekend pack. However, this design is not much good if you are only carrying a little gear and can't pack it tight. It also is a relatively *hot* pack—like all frameless packs—since there is no air circulation between your back and the pack itself. Still, if you cross-country ski, climb or backpack in the cool of the morning this is an excellent choice. The Jensen design is perhaps the best of the lot and the choice of several of my friends.

The internal X-stay or H-stay variant of the Jensen design provides minimum internal support so that partial filling produces an acceptable result. JanSport, Kelty, Sierra Designs, North Face and many others make packs of these types. They are a reasonable compromise between the rigid structure of a frame-bag combination and the freedom of a frameless. Measurements of packs vary somewhat between each maker, so it's important that you try several packs, in several sizes, until you find the one that feels best. The bending of stays in any internal frame pack will make a big difference in the way it rides on your back, so remember this step when you get down to the two or three finalists.

The European Y-frame is really an improvement on the traditional rucksack form. Bergans is probably the biggest maker of these in Europe—Sacs Millet is also good—and both these sacks feature fine European detailing, leather bottoms and ice axe straps. If you avoid the bulb-shaped types and pick a model that holds the weight close to your back, you'll have a comfortable and exceptionally durable pack that's also fine for cross-country skiing and climbing.

Perimeter frame packs in weekender sizes are scaled down versions of frame packs and are usually on the large side. They are a fine choice if you don't plan on cross-country use, and they do carry lots of gear. The Himalayan 9 is representative of this type; it holds a large amount of gear without any problems. It's also excellent for dragging along camera gear if you're the Ansel Adams type.

The Katmandu is one of the new conversion travel packs from Kelty. It features a precontoured internal frame, a lumbar back support and a wrap-around waist strap with a stainless steel buckle. In addition, the Katmandu has a removable top pocket that doubles as a fanny pack. *(Rick Ridgeway)*

From perimeter packs, the logical progression to larger sizes leads to the sack and frame combinations that most backpackers feel they need. The same statements pertinent to weekend packs and their layout and organization are applicable to bags and frames, but there are some additional tests you should try to assure the best results.

The first is a stress test for the frame. Frames, traditionally made from aluminum in alloy, have to stand up to diagonal stress. If you can put one lower corner of the frame on the ground and rest your body weight on the upper corner—after asking permission from the salesman first—you can be sure the frame will stand up to your use. For the most part, frame failure is a thing of the past; one manufacturer, Kelty, even offers a lifetime guarantee.

 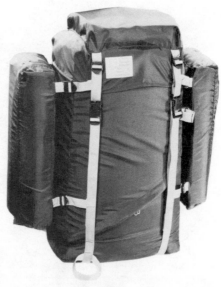

Two more internal frame packs: Kelty's Gendarme (left) has a front access design; it also features a foam laminate waistband, a breathable lumbar support pad and an easily adjusted suspension system. The Gendarme holds 4,000 cubic inches and weighs three pounds, 12 ounces. It retails for $99. The Glacier (right) from Himalayan also features an adjustable support system. It has detachable side pockets and holds 3,972 cubic inches. This four-pound pack sells for $118.

A new and well-tested option is the frame that Coleman offers in their Peak One series. This frame is made from high impact, foamed polyprophlene and flexes with your body. It also has several dozen slots and a system of adjustments that will fit literally anybody who's over five-feet-tall. Since this pack and the several bag options are much less expensive than anyone else's bag, you should look here first. If you don't find this pack workable, go on to the other options.

With packs other than the Coleman you'll find a more limited number of options in fit. Shoulder attachment, length of frame and height of bag attachment are all variables that you'll have to check at the store. What you're looking for is a pack that will carry your load high and close to your body.

The backband that keeps the frame from digging into your back is a very important part of the total system. It should be smooth enough so you can wear your pack against your bare skin on hot days; it should be wide to distribute the load but not so wide that it's uncomfortable; and it should be made of a material, like mesh, that will allow air circulation. You should also check to see that it has an adjustable tensioning system—usually cords or elastic—so you can adjust the backband to the weight you're carrying.

The adjusting system for the straps and hipbelt should have strong webbing and buckles you can adjust without breaking fingernails. Wide is usually best here; heat seal the ends of the straps with a match if they start to ravel with use. Pack lifters can be a worthwhile option if chosen for your specific frame system.

Additional quality indicators on frames include caps, if H-shape tubes are used; reinforcing sections on the joints of tubing; and a system for attaching the bag to the frame that's secure yet easily detachable for cleaning.

Pack bags provide the same choices that you find in weekend packs. The signs of quality are even seams, double stitching at stress spots and an attention to detail that is evident upon close inspection. Divisions and pocket placement are again a matter of choice. It is important that the pocket closure system is secure; nothing is more distressing than back*tracking* to retrieve something that fell out of an open pocket.

Many designs offer a high bag and a lower, open section so you can attach a sleeping bag, Ensolite pad and the like. Closed, lower sections provide more protection for bags with just a slight weight penalty.

Serviceable division systems are as varied as the models of American cars. There is still a lot to be said for the large, undivided sack that provides the biggest possible area for the least weight. It also allows the small item you're looking for to drop to the bottom.

Another major option is the two-space division that has a separate bag on the bottom of the cargo sack for your sleeping gear. Gerry and others offer packs that have a multitude of horizontal divisions that open with individual zippers. Other packs feature zippers around the back that can be opened like a piece of soft luggage. The best of these systems also uses straps for security.

The material that your pack frame bag is made from is probably the *least* important item. Cordura is probably the best choice, but ripstop and other nylons are worthwhile if you're going light. Bag material rarely fails; it's usually the fasteners that let go. One option you should consider is some kind of waterproofing. A good emergency measure here is some gaffer's tape and a small painter's dropcloth packed in the lightest plastic you can find. An eight by ten-foot dropcloth only weighs a few ounces, and you can get two or three pieces out of an 89-cent cloth that will be large enough to cover your pack completely.

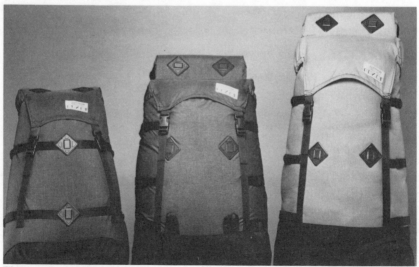

The new Peak 1 line of internal frame packs from Coleman are all top-loading; their main pack bodies are made of Cordura nylon. They each have drawcord closures with contoured storm flaps. Capacity range: 2,850 cubic inches in Model 670; 4,013 in the 680; 5,063 in the 690.

Now you've got the essential information needed to pick your basic pack. You should realize that a weekender or a frame and bag combination won't meet *all* your bag needs. For very short jaunts you're going to need a small rucksack or a waist or "asspack" to carry lunch, camera gear and other items too big for your pockets.

Waist packs free your arms. Unfortunately you can't carry much in a waist pack, and most aren't padded. You'll find an Ensolite lining will make it possible to carry your camera and a couple of extra lenses in a waist pack. Defunct sleeping pads are a good source for this custom option.

Since waist packs and rucksacks are not expensive you can probably afford to have one of each. The waist pack can be used for short jaunts on day hikes while you can use the larger rucksack for all day trips. The same tests of quality in material, workmanship and design that apply to other packs apply here. Don't get one of those cheapo thin nylon packs; they'll lose their straps and be generally uncomfortable for their limited life. Waist packs of quality are made with the same materials as standard packs use, and you can expect to pay only between $15 and $35 for a long-lasting model.

With rucksacks you have more options, since they double as weekend sacks in the higher capacity models. A two-section pack is a recommended option. A rucksack should be usable for short bike trips, cross-country skiing on improved tracks and for toting camera gear and fishing tackle to areas more than a mile from the road.

That about covers the purchase of packs, but there are still a few points you should be aware of. First, don't be afraid to add pockets and other non-structural changes. One of the earmarks of the experienced packer is that he has strong ideas about what he needs and is willing to make changes to reach this ideal. Second, you can save some money by sewing your own frame bags and other packs from kits. This will take you some time, but you'll be able to place pockets wherever you want. Third, you don't have to buy *new* gear. Lots of people find that they've bought the wrong gear and offer it slightly used at good prices. The bulletin boards at mountain shops and around universities are a great source of used, but useable, gear. You can also save money by taking advantage of the season-end sales in October or early November when mountain shops clear their

My mutt's been hounding me for years to get him a well-balanced Doggie Pack.

inventory for winter ski gear. Savings from 20 percent to 40 percent are possible then. Many shops, like North Face in Berkeley, also have seconds for sale. Most of these have only cosmetic flaws; if you're near a manufacturing source, you should certainly check into this for rock-bottom prices. Fourth, in addition to a wide variety of regular packs, you will find many styles to fit special needs—such as small ones for children and double ones for dogs.

The final thing you should know before walking away from this chapter is that no gear is perfect for every use, and even gear you bought a year or two ago may seem outdated by the latest "improvements." Don't worry about that stuff; invest in the best pack you can afford and treat it well and it should last ten or more years. Older gear seems to grow on you after you've fine-tuned the pack to your own desires over the years. So, look at all the gear on the market; try to field-test what you can and then make your choice. The result will be years of comfortable backpacking, a very worthwhile investment.

2 Boots

Nearly every store I pass today seems to have a window full of heavy boots. Hiking, climbing, walking or other specialized footwear for the walker is available in styles and locales never dreamed of before. As more and more of us take to the woods, care of those bony appendages at the ends of our legs becomes of increasing importance. Still, it is within the realm of possibility to hike or backpack wearing just about any kind of footwear, or none at all.

Of course, if that option were so attractive, the market for specialized boots would be rapidly shrinking—instead of expanding. Sure, it's entirely possibly to hike in sneakers or running shoes or sandals. But the end of such a day would bring uncomfortable results: sore, aching, hot feet, with a mass of bad blisters. Added to this will be overtired legs and a generally fatigued body because of the extra exertion necessary to make up for footwear problems.

Remember these results when you're having second thoughts about spending $60 to $100 or more for a pair of good, well-fitted hiking boots.

Much of what is sold to today's backpacker falls into a range of strength, size and weight that is more suitable for the serious rock climber or winter alpinist. Weight, while not the primary consideration in a backpacking or hiking boot, is of great importance. Various estimates of the effect of an overweight hiking boot list the addition of a single pound on the foot as akin to adding five to ten pounds of weight in your pack. Assuming the top estimate to be true, then you're lugging along an extra 20 pounds of pack weight when your boots are only two pounds heavier than they need be. For most trail use with moderate weight pack, a medium weight boot, in a range of about 3 to 4½ pounds, is more than ample. Heavier boots will only punish you, while light shoes will do far too little to protect and support your feet when you're toting a heavy pack over rocky and rough trails.

A New York podiatrist told me: "The extra weight isn't the only reason to avoid extra heavy, extra stiff boots. A lightly loaded hiker will not bend the stiff boot as it should be bent while walking. This lack of flexion leads to fatigue and may cause foot problems."

Boot fit is of paramount importance. A hiking boot should have a bit more toe room than you would expect to find in dress shoes or boots. Again, recommendations vary, but look for one-half to three-quarters of an inch of clearance between your toes and the front of the boot. Since a ruler doesn't fit very well inside the boot once your foot is in there, first jam your foot as far forward in the unlaced boot as it will go. Kick the floor or another solid object to make sure the toes are as far forward as possible. Then stick your index finger down the back of the boot—in higher boots, you'll need something to extend the reach. If the finger goes right down to the sole, the boot is a good fit for you. If it goes only halfway, the boot will be too snug. If two fingers slide on down, you can expect to get a great many abrasion blisters from too large a boot continually sliding back and forth and up and down on your foot. Of course, wear the socks you would normally wear when hiking.

Width for any hiking boot, again with the proper socks on your feet, is not a loose fit. The boot should fit snugly across the widest part of your foot, though you must be careful to avoid a binding tightness.

Boot fit is the single most important consideration when buying new hiking boots, even more important, really, than overall boot quality. A good fitting pair of boots will break in easily, and should serve you well for a long period of time without causing any painful foot problems. A poorly fitted pair of boots may never shape themselves to your feet and will make every hike not only drudgery but often a painful experience. While mail-order fitting is possible, the types of boot lasts used vary widely, making fitting difficult. Thus, no boots should be mail-ordered unless there is a firm return policy should the boots not fit correctly.

Mail-order fitting just about cuts out one chance at improving the fit of boots that are slightly tight: many shops selling supplies for climbers and backpackers have shoe stretching machines. If a boot is an *almost* perfect fit, these machines can be used to move things around enough to fit minor oddities in bone structure. Seldom, if ever, will a shop be willing to use its stretching machine on boots bought elsewhere (and you'll certainly have to buy the boot before they'll do the stretching).

Once proper boot fit is determined, you can go about the process of checking out quality, construction details and weight. Sole construction is probably most people's first consideration. Most heavy-duty and medium-duty hiking boots today use Vibram lug soles. Vibram soles are single piece and come in several weights and designs. But there are alternatives.

Boot selection can be a bit confusing *(Charles Self)*

Browning's Featherweight features a knurled cushion crepe sole—better suited for dayhiking than for rigorous backcountry treks. It sells for about $105. (The Ladies' model is about $10 less.)

The Browning Featherweight is a different type of hiking boot, designed less for heavy-duty backpacking than for woods-prowling with a small daypack. The lugged sole is a crepe material, and the entire boot is much lighter than almost any other hiking boot I've checked, even though the tops are much higher than most. Break-in is almost instantaneous. I spent a full day with these boots on the first time I wore them, walking nearly ten miles. Discomfort was very slight, though I have to admit I was happy to change into a pair of running shoes at day's end.

Actually, the running shoe boom has had a great influence on the entire footwear market. The trend today is toward a more lightweight hiking boot. Companies such as Danner, Donner and Dunham are making strides in this lightweight area. And a company such as New Balance—which made its name solely on running shoes—is now making inroads in the backpacking boot segment.

In addition to the lightweight trend, recent boot innovations include the use of Gore-Tex for watertightness and breathability; and synthetics such as Thinsulate for insulation.

Sole stiffness will often vary greatly between different styles of hiking boot. Some models have extremely stiff soles—almost unbendable by hand—while others are easily bent. The Browning Featherweight, because it's made of crepe, is the most flexible. Perhaps the best choice these days for moderate hiking would be a lightweight boot with a heavy Vibram sole.

When checking sole stiffness, don't just bend and twist with your hands; it's not a true test of flexibility. Many times a boot that seems too stiff when hand-flexed will feel fine on your foot. Always try to walk around as much as possible in any pair of boots you're thinking of buying. The store should provide carpeted areas for this purpose. With mail-order boots, stay on the rugs at home or the company may refuse to accept a return.

Upper quality is sometimes more difficult to determine. Generally, the upper should be made of as few pieces of leather as possible. This is because seams can wear and eventually break open; they also have a strong tendency to leak. Dexter's Milo Sitka—an old reliable—has a single piece of leather, with a heel cap added for greater wear. The Walker Shoe Company puts out a good boot, however, with two-piece construction (plus backstay protector). Both pairs offer quality stitching, using nylon thread, plus double seams at stress points.

Browning boots are of a moccasin design, which entails the use of several pieces of leather (a rough count shows at least three—plus the backstay protector, tongue and toe stiffener). Stitching along the cap of the Brownings is of heavy nylon, while the seams attaching the upper to the base of the shoe (the moccasin part of the base, not the sole) are tripled.

Overall quality in each of the boots mentioned is surprisingly good. The folks at Fabiano, Raichle, Vasque and Red Wing also lay claim to first-rate footwear.

Moving on down the boot once more, we come to the type of welt used to hold the sole to the upper. For hiking, two types of welts serve best. Goodyear welts and Norwegian welts are actually very similar, with the main difference being in the angle of the stitching.

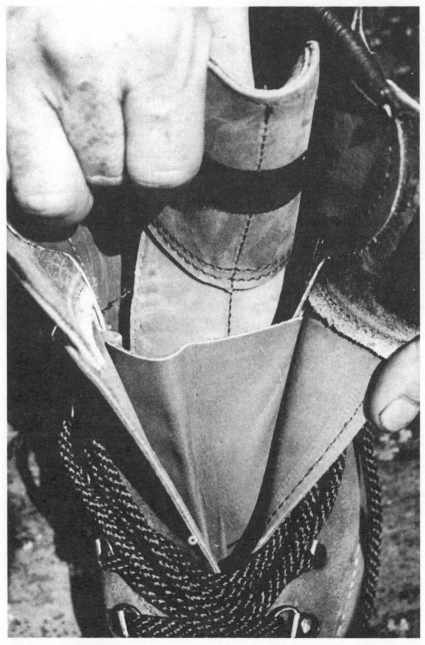

The Milo Sitka uses a many-layered tongue/cover construction with a Velcro strip added to keep the tongue immobile.

Both involve stitching the upper to the inner sole and midsole and the lug sole to the midsole, which produces a strong and functional boot. Injected welts may sometimes be found, and the occasional cemented welt is also sold. Cemented welts are almost invariably shunned, but the type of injected welt which uses a separate midsole offers some advantages, such as no chance of stitching wearing out or deteriorating and no water penetration through needle holes. The choice is up to you and your wallet.

Leather quality in boot construction is also crucial. The boot should be made of top grain leather, which is the top side of the leather as it is split from the full hide. (Leather directly from the cow is much too thick to use as boot uppers, so it must be split before use. The interior splits are not as strong as the top grain splits). It matters little whether the leather is smooth, rough-grained or pebbled. Make certain, though, that the maker of the boot assures you that the rough outside leather used is top grain.

Lacing is close to the final spot in boot selection. Most boots today come with some form of speed lacing. The simplest way to make sure the hooks for the lacing stay intact is to look for those companies that use case-hardened steel in the hooks. In any other case, the standard lacing eyelet is a much better bet from the standpoint of long life and easy replacement when damaged.

Boot break-in is a cause of despair to many people, including this writer. The Brownings took little or no time to break in, but I'm still processing a pair of Milo Sitkas. A friend who prefers jungle boots says he has taken as long as a year to break in a new pair of boots. My breaking-in consists of starting to wear the boots around the house for no more than an hour a day. As this becomes bearable, the time is extended. When the time passes a reasonable mark, say two to three hours, the boots are worn on short walks outdoors, usually for distances of under a mile or two. The distance is extended as the boots begin to feel comfortable. The slower and more carefully the break-in is carried out, the longer the boot should last, and the easier on your feet the process will be.

In cases where new boots must be used at once for a long hike, I can only offer you sympathy and this suggestion: simply put the boots on, stand in a bathtub full of tepid water until the boots are thoroughly soaked and then wear them until they dry, doing as much walking as possible while the boots are drying. At its best, this is an emergency shot, and will be nastily uncomfortable, but it is said to work very well.

Boot care is a simple process. Keep them clean or as clean as possible. Give the leather enough oil to prevent drying out. Dry wet boots slowly after stuffing them with paper. Never place wet boots anywhere near a heat source such as a campfire or radiator.

Now, you may start walking.

3 Sleeping Bags

Today's backpacker is blessed with a vast array of sophisticated equipment designed to make life in the field easier, safer and more comfortable. Some of this equipment is quite useful, and some is mere gadgetry; but none of it is more essential than a good sleeping bag. The backpacker who fails to sleep warmly and well will likely have an unpleasant trip regardless of the beauty of the scenery, the quality of the food or the compatibility of the companions.

Fortunately, more high quality sleeping bags are currently available than ever before. Unfortunately, there are also many low quality bags on the market. Unless you have a basic knowledge of the subject, you stand a good chance of not receiving full value for your dollar. Worse yet, you may end up with a bag that does not deliver the expected performance when it is most needed.

The great number of sleeping bags available can be confusing to the buyer who lacks a little basic knowledge of the subject. *(Engerbretson and Dvorak)*

INSULATION

It must be understood that a sleeping bag functions by providing insulation. That is, it traps the heat produced by the sleeper's body and prevents it from escaping. The better this heat can be retained, the warmer the bag.

Since it has been found that one of the best insulators is immobile air, almost any substance which will create "dead air space" can be an effective insulator—wool, kapok, chicken feathers or even crumpled newspapers. This is not to say, however that any of these materials will make a good sleeping bag. The demands placed upon a backpacker's sleeping bag go well beyond mere insulation.

A sleeping bag must be reasonably lightweight, easily compressible but with the resiliency to return to its original thickness. While it retains body heat, it must "breathe" to allow body moisture to escape. The number of insulating materials which meet these stringent requirements is limited. In fact, for the backpacker, only two materials deserve serious consideration—waterfowl down and polyester fibers.

Waterfowl down—the soft fuzz that lies beneath the bird's feathers, has long been the insulating material used in sleeping bags designed for the coldest temperatures. No other material traps as much dead air, compresses as tightly, lofts as high for its weight or breathes as easily. In short, high quality down is very well suited for use as sleeping bag insulation. The key words, though, are "high quality" down; not all down meets this standard.

The best down is that from mature northern geese. Since most birds being raised for the eating table are killed well before they mature, such down is difficult to obtain. Therefore, manufacturers are often forced to use down of a lower quality, or to which feathers have been added. The feathers have few of the desirable properties of true down.

Some manufacturers of excellent bags have switched from goose down to that taken from mature ducks. They feel that the best duck down is superior to the inferior goose down which is available. The rarity of the best goose down has driven its price to astronomical levels. The use of high-quality duck down allows the price of a sleeping bag to remain fairly reasonable. There is no question that the best goose down is better than the best duck down, but today a top quality bag filled with duck down will likely perform very well for the average backpacker.

Despite some advertising claims, the color of the down has no bearing on its insulating properties. White or gray down performs equally well, though the white is sometimes preferred for cosmetic reasons because it does not show through thin nylon cloth.

Since the down in a sleeping bag is hidden from view, it is difficult to judge its quality. There are few industry standards of quality, and product labeling ranges from reasonably accurate to *down*right misleading. It is truly a case of "let the buyer beware." By law, products labeled as "down" are required to contain at least 80 percent down and down fiber; in a bag labeled "goose down," at least 90 percent of this must be from a goose. Thus, there is a great deal of room for additional feathers and fibers of less desirable characteristics. A bag labeled as "100 percent down," though, must contain *only* down, no feathers. The laws say nothing about the quality of the down, however.

Various manufacturers' claims, such as "prime," "northern," "AA," or "Genuine Great Bear Lake Super Loft Prime Northern Down," are little more than advertising jargon and should be ignored.

Some indication of the feather content of the down can be obtained by squeezing the bag to feel for sharp, stiff feather stems. Even the best down bags will unavoidably contain a few feathers. But if such feathers seem too numerous, look for a different brand of bag. The best rule to follow is to buy only a bag manufactured by a reputable company, and if possible buy from a shop which specializes in backpacking equipment.

The overall quality of workmanship on the visible portion of the bag is generally a good indication of its inner quality. If care has been taken with the stitching, cut of the cloth and finishing details, reasonably good down fill was probably also used. Finally, price is *usually* a good indication of down quality. Down is the most expensive part of the bag; if the sale price is too low it is likely due to the use of inferior filling. There are few bargains in sleeping bags.

Until fairly recently, no serious backpacker would consider anything other than a down filled sleeping bag. Other bags were too heavy and bulky, or they were too skimpy to provide the necessary warmth. However, with the introduction of several quality polyester fibers, the situation has changed. Some backpackers are actually choosing synthetic bags over those filled with down.

Some of these filling materials—such as Celanese PolarGuard, Dupont's Dacron Fiberfill II, Hollofil II and the new Quallofil—are almost as lightweight, have almost as much loft and are almost as compressible as down. Almost, but not quite. Down is still superior in each of these respects. But the polyesters have two advantages over down that make them the preferred choice of many backpackers.

First, the price of a top quality Fiberfill II or PolarGuard bag is much lower than that of a comparable down filled bag. Of even greater importance to those who hike in wet or humid climates is the fact that the polyesters, in contrast to down, do not readily absorb water. They retain a high percentage of their loft—hence their warmth—when they are wet, and they dry in a fraction of the time of down.

The many fine polyester bags now available to backpackers offer an excellent alternative to those who neither require nor can afford a top-of-the-line down filled bag. If you live or hike in wet country, the polyesters should be your first choice regardless of the size of your bankroll.

In addition to the problem of the quality of the insulating material, the unwary buyer is faced with two other confusing and often misleading aspects of sleeping bag "lore"—the weight of the filling and the effective temperature rating of the bag.

While some of the better companies no longer do so, many bags are still identified according to the weight of the insulation they contain. Such designations actually give relatively little information concerning the potential warmth of the bag. The insulating property of any fill material is a function of its thickness or loft, not of its weight. For example, a large rectangular bag containing two pounds of fill will have considerably less loft (i.e., warmth) than a close fitting mummy style bag containing exactly the same weight of insulation.

Rather than the weight of the fill, look for the bag's *loft*. The greater the loft, the greater the potential warmth of the bag. Be alert to the fact, however, that some manufacturers list the loft of the entire bag, while others list only the loft of a single side. The latter

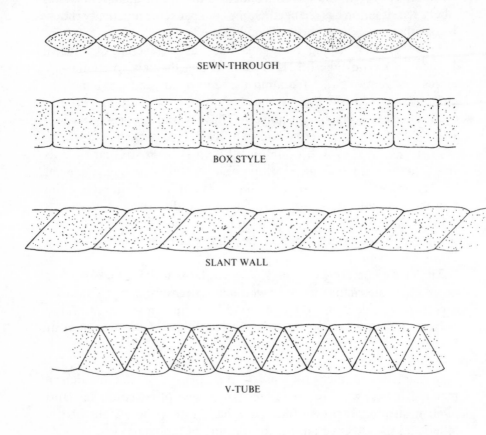

SEWN-THROUGH

BOX STYLE

SLANT WALL

V-TUBE

LAMINATED

SLEEPING BAG BAFFLE CONSTRUCTION

method gives a better indication of the insulating potential of the bag. When the double layer method is used, the figure should be divided by two.

The effective temperature rating of the bag is also a figure that should be approached with some skepticism, particularly if a single figure is stated. "This bag comfortable to minus-10°F," means very little. There are simply too many variables involved to make the figure anything more than a very rough estimate of how warm *you* will be while sleeping in the bag.

The figure fails to consider, for example, whether or not you are sleeping in a shelter, whether there is any wind, what kind of a pad or mattress you are using, what you have eaten before going to sleep, what you are wearing in the bag and how much heat your own metabolism produces. A bag's temperature rating is very nebulous and can be modified by many factors.

BAG CONSTRUCTION

Regardless of whether the bag is insulated with down or one of the polyester fibers, some method of construction must be used to prevent the filling from shifting and creating cold spots. The method used will in part determine the bag's warmth, cost and total weight.

The most simple method is *sewn-through* construction, in which the bag is quilted by sewing the inner and outer shells together to bind the insulation into position. This method is only used on the more inexpensive bags, because wherever a quilt line occurs, the insulation is compressed leaving a cold spot. It is best to avoid bags of this type unless they are to be used for low altitude summer camping or if economy is an overriding consideration.

Down filled bags are usually constructed with a series of *baffles* between the inner and outer shells which permit the bag to maintain a uniform loft with no cold spots at the seams. Such baffles will be either nylon netting (lightweight but rather fragile) or solid nylon cloth (strong but heavier).

In their simplest form, the baffles run vertically between tne shells *(box style construction)*. Some feel that this method is not as efficient in preventing down shift as when the baffles run at angles *(slant wall construction)*. The most efficient method of all, and the one used in

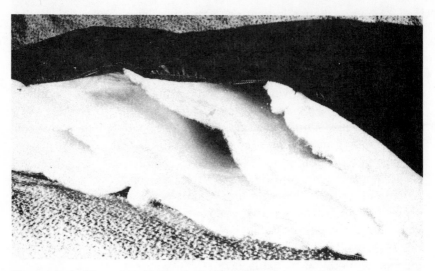

One method of fastening polyester batts (PolarGuard) into a sleeping bag to permit even loft and no sewn-through seams. Note that the batts are sewn along each edge, but only through either the top or the bottom bag shell. Sleeping bag by North Face. *(Engerbretson and Dvorak)*

most of the highest quality bags, is the *V-tube* or *overlapping-V* construction. This method produces a slightly heavier bag and is more time-consuming (and expensive) to manufacture but is extremely effective in producing uniform loft and minimum down shift.

A few bags utilize *laminated construction*; two complete bags with sewn-through seams are joined together with one inside the other so the seams are offset. While efficient, this method requires four shells rather than two; this makes the bag more expensive and quite heavy.

An additional "side-wall" baffle is often used between the shells along the full length of the side of the bag to prevent down from moving between the top and bottom halves. Some manufacturers feel that a side-wall baffle is important to assure even loft, while others believe that the absence of the baffle permits the user to intentionally shift more down to the top when it's needed for extra warmth.

The method of cutting and assembling the inner and outer shells also varies from one manufacturer to another. Some utilize the *differential cut* in which the circumference of the inner bag is less than that of the outer bag. This technique permits the bag to retain a more even loft, since a knee, elbow or other body part cannot compress the inner shell against the outer and create thin, cold spots.

Other manufacturers, however, feel that the differential cut causes the bag to stand away from the sleeper's body in some places and is, therefore, not as warm as a *non-differential* or *space-filler cut* bag which nestles closely to the sleeper. Excellent bags can be made from either method.

BAG STYLES

Several different styles or shapes of backpacking sleeping bags are available, but the most popular is the *mummy bag.* Tapering from a wide shoulder to a narrow foot, the form-fitting mummy bag offers the greatest warmth for the lightest weight. Its narrow shape, however, may prove too confining for some sleepers who prefer a bit more room in which to move around. For such people, the *barrel* or *modified mummy* offers a good compromise between warmth, weight and roominess.

While a few lightweight bags are available with the familiar rectangular shape, they have generally not proven popular with backpackers. Such a bag has too much interior space which must be heated by the body. When compared with a mummy bag of equal

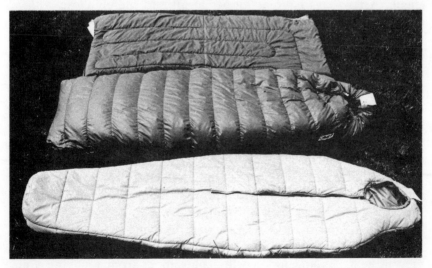

(Top to bottom) Rectangular style, barrel or semi-mummy style, and mummy style sleeping bags. *(Engerbretson and Dvorak)*

45

loft, it will weigh significantly more. In addition, the rectangular bag rarely has an integral hood. All of these factors make the rectangular bag not nearly as warm as the mummy or barrel shape.

BAG FEATURES

Though most backpacking sleeping bags are remarkably similar, the observant shopper will find points of difference in some of their features. Before making your final selection, it is wise to examine a number of bags to compare these features.

Most bags offer an integral hood, which is very important in increasing their warmth. The method of hood closure varies from one brand to another and should be inspected to be certain that the opening can be easily adjusted. Check, too, to see that exposed cords, cord locks, grommets or other hood parts will not rub against your neck or face when the hood is tightly closed. This is best accomplished by actually trying on the bag in the shop.

The length, placement and style of the zipper should also be considered carefully. The zipper will either run down the center of the top or down one side of the bag and may be either partial or full length. A few bags have no zipper at all and merely close with a drawstring around the top.

The full length zipper permits opening of the bag for greater ventilation than the shorter style, an important consideration for summer use, and it will often permit the joining of two bags. Not all bags with a full length zipper can be joined, so check that point if it's important to you. When buying two such bags, be sure that one is a left-hand zipper and the other a right-hand model.

The zipper on most high quality bags will be made of either nylon or plastic rather than metal—which may tend to freeze, jam or break—and the teeth should be large. It should also have a double slide which will allow the bag to be opened from either the top or the bottom for ventilation on a warm night.

Make sure that there is a large, well insulated draft tube or flap running the full length of the zipper on the inside of the bag to prevent heat loss and to keep the cold zipper from touching your skin. A draft tube that is too narrow will be ineffective. A few bags also have some type of fabric stiffener sewn into the draft tube to prevent the zipper teeth from snagging on loose material. This is a very nice feature if you can find it.

Some bags have tie tabs or snaps placed at intervals around the inside for use in securing a liner. The liner can help in keeping the bag clean and will add some degree of warmth. But unless it is fastened very well, a liner tends to tangle easily and can be very uncomfortable. If you think you may use a liner, check the number and placement of the tie downs very carefully.

SELECTING A SLEEPING BAG

Before you actually shop for a bag, decide which style will best meet your needs and what features you will need. Will it be used in the winter or only during the spring, summer and fall? Will it be used mainly in a dry climate, or under humid, rainy conditions? Will down or polyester filling be best for your requirements? How much money are you prepared to invest in a bag?

Once you have some idea of the type of bag you need, you can begin to look through catalogs and visit shops to get a better idea of what is available. Look at as many bags as possible to compare features, construction and prices.Carefully inspect the details discussed earlier, and pay particular attention to the workmanship—the quality of the stitching, the shell fabric and the general design. In the case of a down filled bag, be sure that the fabric is of a tight weave that does not let the down fibers escape. Be willing to pay a little more to obtain a bag that will give good service for many years rather than try to save a few dollars and end up with an inferior product that will not live up to your expectations.

At the same time, don't make the common mistake of buying "too much bag." Hikers are often advised to select a bag that will be suitable for the most severe conditions under which it will be used. If this is done, however, the bag will be too warm for more normal conditions, and the extra expense will not be justified. It is better to buy a bag which is adequate for the conditions under which it will be most often used. Then, when more severe conditions dictate, it can be used with a liner and/or a cover, and you can sleep in more clothing to increase its temperature range.

When choosing a bag, actually get into it in the shop to be certain that it is long enough and is comfortable. Check the ease with which the zipper and the hood can be opened and closed. These details cannot be evaluated when making a catalog purchase, so try to shop for the bag in person. If this cannot be done, check these points as soon as it is received so it can be returned if all is not right.

You may also wish to consider sewing your own bag from one of the many kits now available. Almost any style is produced in kit form with either down or polyester insulation; the odds are very good that you will be able to find exactly what you are looking for. Such kits are time-consuming to construct, but while previous sewing experience is helpful, it is not necessary. If care is taken, the end result will be a first class bag at a considerable saving in price.

Incidentally, several kit manufacturers feature children's bags that can be sewn into a short size, and as the child grows, they can be easily extended to provide the proper fit. In this way, the child can have the advantage of a good bag that will never be outgrown, another economy consideration.

SLEEPING BAG CARE

The proper care of a sleeping bag can be summed up in two words—*clean* and *dry*. Dirt and moisture are your bag's worst enemies.

Common sense precautions are all that are necessary to keep your bag clean. Use a ground cloth or a poncho under it, and don't climb into it while wearing filthy trail clothes. A liner may help keep the inside of the bag clean.

Whenever possible, drape the bag over a dry branch or your tent to air it out before packing it away after each use, and give it a thorough airing when you arrive home. The bag will collect a great deal of body moisture during the night, and unless this is removed it will accumulate and reduce the bag's insulating efficiency considerably. Of course, any bag that has been soaked by rain, snow or other moisture should be completely dried out as soon as possible.

When your bag eventually becomes too dirty for comfort, it can be either washed or dry cleaned. If the bag is to be dry cleaned, be certain that the cleaner selected has had experience with sleeping bags. If possible, check with a local backpacking shop for recommendations on a dry cleaning establishment that can be trusted with your bag. Then, as a final precaution, ask the cleaner what type of cleaning agent he will use. Only a mild petroleum-based fluid such as Stoddard Solvent should be used. The chlorinated hydrocarbons used for most dry cleaning will ruin a down bag. (The most common fluid of this type is called perchloroethylene or "perk." It should never be used on a bag.)

Following dry cleaning, the bag must be aired out very thoroughly before using it. Hang it outside for several days or a week if necessary to remove *all* traces of the smell of the cleaning fluid. If this is not done, the residual fluid could cause skin rashes, brain damage or even death. I exaggerate not. Take no chances.

Though improper hand washing can ruin a bag, this may still be the safest cleaning method. Use mild soap such as Ivory, since harsh detergents will remove the natural oils from down; do the job by hand in the bathtub rather than a washing machine. Gently knead warm, soapy water through the bag being careful not to wring or twist it—which will damage the internal baffles. For this same reason, never pick up a soaking wet sleeping bag. Wet insulation is very heavy and can easily rip the baffles or tear loose the stitching of a polyester filled bag.

When the bag has been completely washed, drain the tub and rinse it several times, again by gentle kneading. Continue to drain the tub, and add clean water until no more soap suds can be removed from the bag. Then very gently *press* as much water as possible from the bag, but do not wring it out. Gather it completely in your arms so all of its weight is supported, and carry it to your dryer. Set the dryer to the lowest heat setting, and run the bag through as many cycles as necessary to completely dry it. It is a good idea to place a pair of laceless sneakers into the dryer with the bag as they will bounce around and break up the wet clumps of insulation. When the bag seems dry, hang it outside in the sun for a final airing.

When being packed for a trip, the bag can be jammed at random into a stuff bag rather than folded and rolled methodically, but care should be taken when removing it from the stuff bag so the baffles are not ripped. Pull it out gently in large clumps rather than simply tugging at one end. When stored at home between trips, the bag should *not* be kept in the stuff sack but in a large box or other container which will let the insulation expand.

A modern sleeping bag is a wondrous thing. Buy a good one, treat it with respect, and you'll be rewarded by many nights of warm, restful sleep.

Browning's Wind River II mummy bag is rated to minus 15° F. It's insulated with Hollofil II, weighs five pounds, eight ounces and sells for about $155.

Cannondale's Blue Ridge Rider is rated down to 25° F. This modified mummy features differential cut, offset quilting and Hollofil II insulation. It weighs three pounds, eight ounces and retails for about $100.

Himalayan's Bigfoot is a rare center-zip mummy. It's filled with PolarGuard and made of 1.9 ripstop nylon (lining and shell). The bag sells for about $145.

This tapered mummy bag from Kelty features an innovative combination of Quallofil and Texolite. (Texolite is a vacuum-plated polyurethane film supported on a nylon netting that protects the body from radiant heat loss.) The Minaret is rated down to 0° F and weighs four pounds, two ounces.

4 Tents

The type of tent that you should consider depends, of course, on the type of hiking that you do. If most of your backpacking takes place in summer, you can ignore the frostliners. If, however, you spend most of your time above timberline, there is little need for mosquito netting.

A perfect tent should meet these criteria: It should be able to withstand a blizzard comfortably (you and *it*); it should provide a commodious sleeping area in hot, muggy badlands; and, most important of all, it should be *light*.

If such a tent exists, I have never seen it. Which leaves us with a choice of compromises. There are two major categories, with infinite variations. Warm weather tents are designed for use at lower altitudes in, surprise, milder weather. More warm weather tents are sold because more people go hiking in warmer weather. The other type is a cold weather or Alpine tent, geared for higher elevations and snow.

Most of the tents mentioned in this chapter are warm-weather (two to three-season) models. If you are considering extremely high altitudes, you should contact one of the firms that specializes in custom equipment. For us hiking hackers, the tents mentioned here—which are representative of what's available on the market—should be serviceable for backpacking in virtually all areas of the United States.

All of the tents delineated in this chapter are made from one of two types of nylon: taffeta and ripstop. Taffeta nylon is a flat-weave fabric that comes in several thicknesses. When coated with polyurethane, to make it waterproof, it can have a tear strength of up to 50 pounds. Ripstop nylon is a weave that has extra-heavy threads woven in at about ¼-inch intervals to stop tears from running. These threads also help to distribute fabric stress.

Ripstop nylon is the lighter of the two weaves but not necessarily of better quality or more durability. Many tentmakers use a combination of the two nylons to achieve a finished product with special qualities (waterproofness *and* breathability, for example). To check for ripstop, look at the fabric for extra-heavy threads. If you don't see any, the nylon is taffeta. The perfect tent would, of course, have no seams. Instead, the manufacturers have reached another compromise: a flat fell seam. This seems to be the one type of seam that will not blow apart on some windy night.

The thread used in sewing tent seams is also important because it will affect the waterproofness of the seam. Nylon thread is the strongest. Since a needle makes a hole in the tent while sewing, these

Wenzel's tepee-style trail tent is seven feet, four inches tall.

Kelty's Summer Breeze weighs four pounds, five ounces (with fiberglass poles).

spaces must be sealed. If not, rain water will slide down the sides of the tent, through the holes and into the tent. If your tent is sewn with nylon thread, make sure the seams are properly sealed. Sealer will also wear off after some use and must be reapplied. You can recoat your seams with an appropriate sealer, or you can even use airplane glue or rubber cement. I recommend the latter two only in a pinch.

There is another type of thread being used with greater frequency by quality tent manufacturers: Dacron core with cotton wrap. The advantage of using cotton in sewing seams is that when the thread gets wet it expands and fills the thread holes. Old tents were sewn with cotton thread and were quite waterproof for this reason. Unfortunately, these tents were also prone to mildew. The combination of Dacron and cotton is a contemporary solution to the leaky seam problem. Just make sure your tent is bone dry before you pack it away for storage.

Stitching is as important as thread. Lines should be straight, even, and not too close to the edge of the fabric. Higher quality tents will have more stitches per inch, up to ten. Some tents will only have a stitch count of four or five per inch. Another point to consider is that better quality tents will have at least a double line of stitches where fabric stress is most susceptible.

The best way to handle stress in seams, pegs, pole loops and grommets is to reinforce the area. This is often accomplished by sewing an additional piece of nylon over the area and then attaching the loop or grommet. Some tentmakers use the strongest reinforcement possible: nylon webbed strap or tape. These straps or tape are sewn onto possible stress areas—such as guy line points—to help distribute any pull over a larger area.

Ventilation is a necessity in any tent, under any weather conditions. While you sleep, you can give off about a pint of moisture. If you have open vents in your tent, this moisture will not be a problem. If you do not have vents, you will be in for an uncomfortable, muggy night. Most tentmakers have realized that a tent must be well-ventilated; they have added vents at the top or sides or have clever zipper setups in the doors. The tent you're considering should have some type of venting system with mosquito netting to help moisture escape.

Coleman's Peak 1 line features the domed-topped Alpha tents.

The special feature on Cannondale's Wabash is an integral fly design.

Poles and pegs are often overlooked. You should give substantial thought to these supports. Many companies now put shock cords through each pole, thus keeping pole sections together. The addition of shock cords make assembling poles a simple, flip-of-the-wrist maneuver. Pegs come in an assortment of sizes, shapes and materials. I feel that the best all-around type of peg is the U-shaped aluminum peg. It holds better (even in snow) because it is, in effect, two pegs in one. Special conditions require special pegs.

The following tents are a representative sampling of different design and construction modes. They were chosen more or less at random; many have been field-tested. All are recommended. But you must decide which one is the most compatible for your particular needs.

CANNONDALE—WABASH

The innovative feature on the entire line of backpacking tents from Cannondale is the integral fly design: the water-repellent outer wall is part of the tent. The support poles go through sleeves sewn into the fly—with the breathable interior walls suspended six inches below.

This design's effectiveness is two-fold: 1) Rain hits outer wall and rolls off—without touching inner wall; 2) moisture from inside (generated from individuals) passes through both walls, thereby reducing condensation.

The Wabash is a two-person tent that weighs eight pounds, 12 ounces. Additional features include tub floors, fine mesh screen, shockcorded pole assemblies and YKK nylon coil zippers throughout.

Suggested retail price is $295.

COLEMAN PEAK 1—OMEGA

The first four-season tent in the Peak 1 line, it's designed to offer wind resistance and shed heavy snow and rain. This seven-pound, two-ounce dome sleeps up to three persons.

Featherlite poles are made of a composite of graphite, glass fibers and epoxy. All are shockcorded.

The freestanding Omega's tent wall is made of 1.6-ounce uncoated nylon taffeta. Its fly is 1.9-ounce, urethane-coated ripstop nylon. The waterproof floor, also 1.9 ripstop, has 14 inches of wrap to ward off rain and snow. Two triangular windows provide cross-ventilation. The windows and the 36 by 39-inch rectangular door have no-see-um netting.

The Omega is the first four-season tent in Coleman's Peak 1 line.

JANSPORT—YELLOWSTONE

This three-season tent is more than ample for two people. Its total weight is six pounds, three ounces. Center height is 41 inches; floor size is 77 by 94 inches.

Aluminum poles are pre-shockcorded and slide through continuous pole sleeves; they're anchored by grommets in the nylon webbing. The nylon mesh in the covered rear window facilitates ventilation, even with the rainfly on. Additional features include a two-way zippered door with mesh backing; stretch mesh panels between the pole sleeves and the tent canopy; and a clothesline in the tent ceiling.

The Yellowstone is made of 1.9-ounce ripstop nylon; its tub floor and rainfly is constructed of 2.2-ounce coated taffeta. Poles, stakes and rainfly all fit into stuff sack; seam sealer is included.

This tent sells for about $225.

KELTY—ORIZABA

This four-person dome style tent is the largest in the new Kelty line. At 13 pounds, 14 ounces, it's suited more for large groups and expeditions rather than a two-person jaunt into your local wilds.

The Orizaba's unique "crossed rectangle" floor enables each of the four people in the tent to enjoy his or her own bay window view from the comfort of a sleeping bag. The windows as well as the entrance are protected by no-see-um insect netting. The fly is elasticized and has high-wind guylines. The tent comes with shockcorded aluminum poles; but you can order fiberglass poles with graphite ferrules if you desire added strength.

The tub floor is made of three-ounce coated taffeta. Center height measures in at 51 inches.

NORTH FACE—SIERRA

This two-person A-frame has been around for awhile. The poles, made of shockcorded sections of aluminum alloy, fit into the sewn-in grommets at the tent base. The A-frames are 48 inches high; the front and rear guylines run over the top—enabling the structure to withstand blustery mountain winds.

The tub floor is made of 2.8-ounce urethane-coated nylon; it extends 15 inches up the side walls. Double pullouts on either side increase the interior space. The flysheet is made of 2.2 urethane-coated ripstop.

The Sierra is sewn with lap-felled double-needle seams. Stakes, seam sealer and all necessary cords are included. Total weight is seven pounds, six ounces; it retails for $270.

WHITE STAG—STAR DOME

This geodesic four-person tent features a double vestibule with front and rear doors. These are tunnel-style doors with nylon-zippered netting and storm flap. There's a window in both front and rear doors.

The frame is shockcorded fiberglass. The wall is made of breathable nylon, and the floor is coated with nylon. Center height is an adequate four feet. Total weight: nine pounds, 9½ ounces.

WHITE STAG—STAR GAZER

This ultralight model is six pounds lighter than the Star Dome. Its exact weight is three pounds, eight ounces. The Star Gazer will sleep one comfortably—and two intimately.

The door is oval-shaped with a nylon coil zipper around it. There are two windows—at the door and at the body of the tent. The frame is two sectional fiberglass poles. The wall is coated nylon taffeta, and the floor

Kelty's Orizaba weighs a substantial 13 pounds, 14 ounces—making it more suitable for expeditions than for weekend jaunts.

White Stag's Star Dome weighs in at nearly ten pounds.

is polyurethane-coated nylon. Center height is a cozy 23 inches.

You really can't go too far wrong with any well-made tent. If possible, try to rent the tent you want before you come to a final purchase decision. If renting is not feasible, find someone who owns the tent you want, or ask the dealer to set it up so you can at least check it over. In any case, look over seams, zippers, stitching, rainfly, poles and pegs *before you buy.*

While most tentmakers have excelled in the design department, I have found most fail to provide decent "setup" directions. When you finally decide on a tent, make sure you have a set of directions to help you set it up properly. Otherwise you could put undue stress and tension on the wrong area and do some slight but permanent damage to tent cloth or structure. Ask the salesperson to set it up for you, so you'll know exactly what you're buying and also how the damn thing works.

It's your money well-spent for a well-made tent.

White Stag's Star Gazer weighs less than four pounds.

Browning's Hunderwear is another alternative for cold weather: two layers of material leave a dead air insulating space between them.

5 Clothing

Colin Fletcher, in *The Complete Walker,* advocates complete nakedness as the ideal hiking outfit. From this point of view, we add on. We start with underclothing and proceed to stuff our packs full of extras, weighing ourselves down with enough clothing to survive an assault on Mt. Everest (or at least Mt. Whitney).

Even the experienced backpacker will cart along a *bit* too much. And that's fine; it helps to be prepared for a few eventualities. But inexperienced backpackers often end up carrying too much extra baggage. Before dusk arrives, fatigue sets in. Careful layering of clothing can help prevent overloading, providing the most comfort with the least weight.

UNDERCLOTHING

Generally, two sets of underclothing for normal weather are sufficient—allowing one set to be washed while the other is worn. I prefer jockey shorts of cotton rather than the fancier, synthetic briefs; crotch-binding boxer shorts might be a better bet. Unfortunately, women backpackers don't have the same range of choices; but I do recommend cotton.

Depending on the season you may wish to take only one or two T shirts. They're fine for cool mornings and evenings but are not essential in warm weather. They *will* help absorb perspiration and might hold the dampness long enough to help you cool down a bit.

For winter use, you have a choice of innumerable kinds of underwear. For extremely severe weather, down insulated long johns are suitable; for normal cold weather, down is too much. Fisherman, or open weave, knits are more effective and more flexible when used with layered outer clothing. These open weave knits are ideal for the times when the weather suddenly warms up. Simply pull off your jacket, open your shirt and let your body cool down as you quickly lose the insulating effect of those holes in the open weave. Incidentally, if you do select open weave—short or long sleeved— undershirts, make certain that they're the kind with solid shoulder yokes. The waffle weave can be quite painful when pack straps ride on it for any length of time.

Fit of underclothing is very important. Jockey shorts should fit snugly, but other undergarments must fit with enough looseness to prevent binding; they cannot be so loose that they bind up in your outer clothing. This applies to T shirts to some degree but becomes most important with long legged union-suit styles and long sleeved undershirts.

Women should apply the same basic rules to their underclothing: cotton briefs with a snug fit and moderately loose long underwear.

Cotton is preferred over the various synthetics since it is more comfortable against the skin during sweat producing activities. The wicking action of cotton—and wool—is much better than that of nylon, which sort of just lies against your skin soggily after getting wet. The nylon may dry a lot more quickly than the cotton, but it feels much worse.

FIRST OUTER LAYER

The first outer layer of clothing is made up of pants and shirt (we'll toss in socks here, too). The selection of pants suitable for backpacking is quite extensive. Stylistic preferences vary a great deal; the activity, the weather and the terrain should be more important than any considerations of just style.

All hiking pants, whether long or shortlegged, need to be of sturdy, long-lasting material with well-sewn seams and heavy-duty zippers or buttons. Sturdiness serves a double purpose. First, you'll be sitting on the ground, on logs and on rocks much of the time. This tends to provide a sandpaper action that will have your underwear peeking through lightweight britches in no time. Second, you don't want to lug along any more weight than is essential. One good, heavy duty pair of pants can save the weight of an extra insurance pair of lighter weight pants.

If the weather is very warm, a switch to shorts can be a help. In hot weather, I prefer a heavy duty fabric with a more open weave than usual in long legged pants. Much of the area in which I usually hike is full of brambles and small insects, both of which can provide great discomfort with shorts.

Pants fit is as important as underwear fit. Here, style enters into it. As much as I enjoy wearing dungarees around the house and office, I don't normally wear them on the trail. The fit is just too quick, causing binding in the legs, seat and crotch. Pick a pair of pants that fit loosely and give sufficient freedom of movement to your legs. Sturdy belt loops are a must, as is a good, heavy belt (or suspenders if you prefer). Waist fit should be looser than usual; your body will settle a bit under the load of a pack, causing your stomach to expand slightly (how much will depend on your physical condition and your general body structure).

Shirts suitable for backpacking vary so much that a selection for any season is very easy. Select a sturdy shirt—as you would pants—for woods and trail wear, and select one that suits the season. On warm days I prefer to start the day with a lightweight cotton chambray shirt with snap fasteners for a variety of reasons; the snaps are easy to fasten (I'm lazy), and a light shirt is a good base for sweaters or other types of outer clothing layers if it gets cooler. Also, the chambray cowboy shirts are available in all sizes, something that can't be said for many of the other available hunting and hiking shirts. For most people, size won't be a problem. If you need a tall size, however, you'll have considerable difficulty finding one. The average-size person can opt for any comfortable shirt made—including corduroy, wool, chamois, plain cotton or a cotton blend. Avoid straight synthetics, though a blend of cotton and a synthetic can keep a shirt looking neat even after several days in the woods.

Look for two breast pockets, solidly-sewn buttons and carefully stitched seams. And make that stitching check a close one.

Socks are not too much of a problem for the backpacker. There are a variety on the market; even novice hikers realize that a good, heavy boot sock is essential to comfortable progress during a long day. Underliner socks—made of silk or cotton for those who dislike the feel of wool—can provide extra warmth on cold days (the cotton sock is better for warmth). For greater warmth on the lower legs, get an over-the-calf or knee-length sock. If you can't locate suitable knee-length socks, go to your local motorcycle dealer, and pick up a pair of motocross socks. These are made for racers and are sturdy and comfortable. My preference for all-round boot wear is the Ragg style sock, as sold by L. L. Bean, Sierra Designs and others. With 85 percent wool supported by 15 percent nylon, it provides what I feel is just the right weight and bulk, along with two lengths to allow some adjustment for the weather. Suitable for any climate, the wool serves to wick off perspiration and keep your feet fairly comfortable even on hot days. They sell for about $7.50 a pair.

Browning's lightweight Rain Coat is made of polyerethane-coated nylon. A popular feature is that the drawstring hood can be concealed inside the collar.

BOOTS

Boots can also be classified as a first layer of outerwear, but they are also the single most important item in anyone's hiking outfit. For that reason, an entire chapter has been devoted to the ramifications of boot wear. Enough said. See Chapter 2.

COOL WEATHER LAYER

Cool weather clothing ranges from a simple pullover sweater to more sophisticated, lightweight down garments and a variety of raingear. Probably of greatest importance is the rainwear.

Select a poncho that is made of good, sturdy material—such as coated nylon—and one that has a hood. The poncho should be bright colored— for a couple of reasons. Safety is first—during hunting season; and secondly, a poncho can be used as a signalling device if you're in trouble.

The best rain fabric choice is probably Gore-Tex, because it's both waterproof and breathable; it's also expensive. More details are given in Chapter 13.

Sweaters for backpacking should be of moderate to heavyweight wool, with preference given to the untreated natural wools that retain water-repelling oils. They might just save you having to dig out the poncho on a few occasions. Turtlenecks are generally too warm in moderately cool weather but are fine for cold weather.

Several types of wool overshirts are available; they can prove handy on a sometime basis (because of their $30-plus price tags, it would be nice to have some other use for them, too). The wool Stag shirt has a double shoulder thickness and makes a comfortable jacket for cool weather. Slightly lighter—and cheaper—is the Alaskan shirt. Both are excellent.

Vests afford freedom of movement and extra warmth in moderately chill weather; they make a fine additional underlayer for very cold weather. Down filled vests are now to be found in just about every line, and most makers now also offer the less expensive synthetic fills that are easier to care for. North Face, among others, also makes a *fleece* vest—which many advocate for damp, chilly climes. North Face's 14-ounce Polarfleece vest is wind-resistant and breathable; the sizing is stylishly snug.

Down sweaters—actually lightweight jackets—are a bit newer than the vests; they provide another good source of warmth for the layer system. While the freedom of movement is a bit less than that with a vest, the longer bodies and the long sleeves aid heat retention. The weight is a bit higher; Sierra Design's sweater, for example, comes in at about 21 ounces, while their quilted vest weighs only 12 ounces. Price differential is commensurate.

The fill is of great importance. Prime goose down is the old insulating favorite for sleeping bags, vests, parkas and so on. Down fills a greater volume for a given weight than any other type of fill, thus providing greater loft and insulation at a very low weight. Price is high, though. Oddly enough, Red China is the major exporter of goose down in the world, but they've cut *down* on shipments lately. As the price of tea in China goes, so goes the price of down.

The major problems with down involve cleaning and wet condition performance. For dry cleaning, if anything other than a very mild solvent is used, the down will be ruined. For hand washing, which is recommended in most cases, a very mild soap needs to be used. Care must be taken to keep from destroying the baffling that is used to keep the down from matting and lumping. Wet weather performance is not good: down mats and loses its loft when wet.

Synthetic fibers such as PolarGuard, Fiberfill and Thinsulate are almost as efficient as down insulation, but a bit more weight must be used to provide the same insulation value. Since these synthetics don't absorb moisture, they don't mat and are much more efficient under wet camping conditions, providing a cushiony feeling even when moderately damp. Synthetics also dry a good deal faster than does down, but they cannot be drycleaned and should only be washed in lukewarm water, without machine agitation. Synthetics are virtually always cheaper than down-filled gear. See also Chapter 3 on sleeping bags.

OUTER LAYERS

When cold weather strikes, consider such things as heavier, exterior wear layers, parkas and down-filled jackets. While backpackers will seldom have the need for insulated leggings to go with the parkas, a good middleweight down- or synthetic-filled parka can

Browning's Western vest is filled with down; its shell is made of Antron nylon.

Cannondale's lightweight Summit vest is insulated with Hollofil II; its shell is also Antron nylon.

make a very late fall or early spring hike a lot more enjoyable. It is seldom necessary to go to the heavyweight expedition styles; the near constant movement on the trail, along with inner layers of clothing, will supply as much warmth as needed. Should you stop for long and start to chill down, you can always pull out your sleeping bag and wrap up in that. There is really no need in carrying more weight than is necessary for basic comfort while on the move. If you're going to be out overnight, that sleeping bag is always there as an added body warmer when the need arises.

Parkas come in many styles—some down filled, others wool lined, some both, some with little or no lining, some waterproof, others nearly so and some using synthetics as a filler material. Average weights can vary widely. JanSport's down-filled Chelan weighs one pound, 12 ounces. North Face's down-filled Serow weighs two pounds, ten ounces—while its Bison synthetic version, insulated with Hollofil II, weighs three pounds, four ounces.

When buying a parka or any outer jacket, keep in mind the ventilation possibilities. Snaps should hold a storm flap over the full

69

length of zipper. Snap or Velcro fasteners at the cuffs are also a big help. Look, too, for a high neck. You can lose an amazing amount of heat energy with an exposed neck; while scarves are handy to carry along, they have a tendency to slip about when you're exerting yourself. Either the waist or hip of the parka should have a closure of some kind; the drawstring is the simplest and most efficient.

Several shell materials are used for parkas; most are made of ripstop nylon or a nylon/cotton blend. Ripstop nylon is identified by the strengthening threads sewn into the fabric in a grid pattern. Blends are usually identified with figures: 60/40 translates to 60 percent cotton and 40 percent nylon.

Stitching in the shell is important. If less than eight stitches per inch are used, the seam will be weak. More than ten stitches will tend to weaken the fabric because of excessive penetration.

Outerwear color is a matter of choice, but some consideration needs to be given to the time of year when such garments are worn. Fall is hunting season in most areas of the country. Bright colors, such as yellow or international orange may help some of the more incompetent hunters in the woods distinguish you from a member of the local deer herd.

HATS

I prefer a hood on the jacket or parka to a hat, though a light hat can do a lot to protect your head on a rainy or hot day. Also, much heat can be lost from the head on a cold day; hoods and hats then become welcome additions. Something on the order of the roller crusher hat is nearly ideal; the oiled felt will keep the head dry and warm, and the hat can be crushed and stuffed in a pocket when it isn't needed. Again, watch those colors, select a bright one for any hunting season hiking.

In general, dealing with a reputable manufacturer or distributor, of which there are a great many now, will help assure you of good quality over a wide line of backpacking clothing. The cost may seem high at the outset, but with it you get years of use, usually troublefree, and good fit and comfort. Once you've got the fit, and paid the price, you need only remember: keep it simple and keep it light.

6 *Accessories*

To say that backpacking is a gadgeteers' sport is a ludicrous understatement. A quick glance in any hiking shop or specialty catalog is quite enough to confuse the beginner as well as the experienced hiker. After the necessary items such as pack, frame, sleeping bag, kitchen equipment and boots, there are endless rows of plastic bottles, foam pads, compasses, flashlights, knives (pocket and belt) and on and on, *ad infinitum*; often, *ad nauseam*. You begin to wonder if you should buy a pack horse to carry all of this seemingly necessary gear. Only experience can teach you what you will need, but there should be some guidelines in the beginning. There are, and that's the point of this chapter.

Over the past few years, I have developed certain criteria for judging the usefulness of an accessory. First of all, I define an accessory as any item other than a pack and frame, boots, sleeping bag, tent, stove, cook pot, spoon and a few personal items such as toilet articles and clothing. There are other necessary items, to be sure, but just about every other piece of gear should, ideally, have at least two uses.

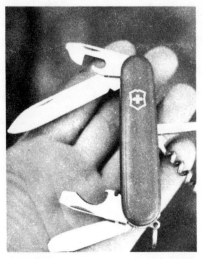 

The Swiss Officer's Knife is one of the more utilitarian pocket knives. *(Don Geary)*

The pot gripper in action *(Don Geary)*

For example, I carry a knife in my pocket—a Swiss Officer's Knife. There are several different models to choose from. I have one with two cutting blades, can opener, bottle opener, screwdriver, punch and corkscrew. Even at home I use the corkscrew to open an occasional bottle of Beaujolais. The cost is around 30 dollars, at any quality backpacking equipment shop.

Another useful item is a pot gripper. If you have ever tried to stir the contents of a pot while it sits atop a small hiking stove, you can easily appreciate the value of one of the little gadgets. The pot gripper works very much the same as a small pair of pliers, which I used to carry before I discovered this handy little tool. A pot gripper will enable you to pick up a hot, heavy pot and pour the contents. These grippers will also convert a pot lid into a frying pan.

Kitchen and cooking gadgets are probably the most numerous. On a recent visit to an equipment shop, I noticed that there were no fewer than ten different types of knife, fork and spoon combination sets. One set even had two spoons—table and tea. I have found it considerably easier to carry just a spoon. Anything that has to be eaten, stirred or mixed can be done with one spoon. I have even become adept at using the spoon as an impromptu spatula.

Some hikers carry two or more cups; I carry one Sierra Cup. It will hold exactly ten ounces of liquid, so it plays an important role in measuring water for freeze-dried meals. The Sierra Cup is twin tempered; the lower portion remains hot, while the upper cools quickly and, therefore, is less likely to burn lips.

There is one piece of equipment that never ceases to amaze and amuse me: the egg carrier. This is a plastic (though some models are aluminum) container that will, ostensibly hold and protect from one to a dozen eggs. Many models have a handle that makes the whole affair look like a miniature suitcase for a traveling chicken. I must confess that I did buy one of these little suitcases years ago but only used it a few times; then I discovered powdered eggs, in crushable packages.

One thing you can be certain of when hiking in the outdoors is that you will get dirty; so will kitchen equipment. And your teeth need to be cleaned, your body washed; socks and other clothing will also benefit from a quick scrubbing. I recently discovered an all purpose cleaner that can be used for just about every type of cleaning—from cook pot to teeth, socks to hair, even shaving cream. Travel-Scrub is made by the Hobson Company in California, and it

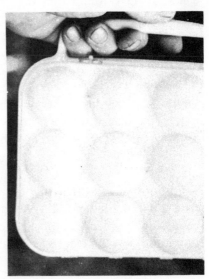

The Sierra cup *(Don Geary)*

The plastic egg carrier, suitcase for chickens *(Don Geary)*

really does serve as an all purpose cleaner. It is also biodegradable. This concentrated all purpose cleaner comes in a two-ounce squeeze container that is more than enough for one week of washing. Current cost is under two dollars per container.

Another handy item is a bandanna. Besides the obvious uses—such as a handkerchief, headband and towel—I also saturate a bandanna with insect repellent and tie it around my neck to keep off biting insects. Other uses include dishrag, cleaning cloth and cold compress (when soaked in water). I always carry three bandannas, rinsing the used and dirty ones and hanging them on the back of the pack to dry. Current cost is about $1.50 apiece.

For sleeping comfort, insulation from the hard ground and a soft seat in rock country, I always carry an Ensolite pad. Actually, Ensolite is the name commonly used for all types of closed cell foam pads. With thicknesses ranging from 3/16 to 3/8 of an inch, they aren't as comfortable as your mattress at home, but they will insulate you from the cold ground. They cost around ten bucks, worth every penny.

It's always a good idea to have some waterproof matches along on a hike. I have found that regular book matches pick up dampness readily. The best solution is to carry waterproof wooden matches. I usually waterproof my own. I first melt down a chunk of paraffin in a tin can. When it is hot, I dip the tips of these matches into the hot wax and lay them out on a sheet of newspaper to dry and harden. After that, I carry the waterproof matches in a small tin box (the kind that throat lozenges come in); they've worked every time.

If you don't want to bother with all this melting, dipping and drying, you can buy matches that have already been treated. One company—Coghlan's from Australia—seems to have cornered the market. They also sell a match that is both waterproof and windproof. These little torches are about an inch and one-half long with the match head taking up about half the stick. I'd bet that you could light a cigarette in a gale wind with one of these matches, providing that the cigarette doesn't blow out of your mouth.

I almost always take a camera along on hikes. Because sunrises and sunsets take place in other than ideal lighting, I use a little gizmo

Camera clamp is a useful accessory from L. L. Bean *(Don Geary)*

The backpackers' pennywhistle (guitar) weighs eight ounces.

with a swivel head, a camera clamp, that will fit any camera that can be used with a tripod. I got mine from L.L. Bean years ago for four dollars. I am reasonably certain that without this little two-ounce wonder, I would have missed many photographs in poor lighting.

There are hiking friends of mine who can't bear to be without *music*— even for a couple of days. A radio would be out of the question—too much of a technological intrusion. What to do? I used to carry a kazoo—but my hiking companions threatened me with bodily harm if I *played* it. Since I couldn't find a *second* use for it, I left it home. Recently, I met a fellow who makes backpackers' guitars. Actually, he calls the eight-ounce model a pennywhistle—and he sells it for a relatively light-weight $65. This fellow, Bob McNally, also makes a weightier two-pound guitar—at a heftier price (about $200). If you're interested, write to him at: McNally Instruments, 1011 Main St., Boonton, NJ 07005. What about a second use for a guitar? If you ever get stuck on a river without a paddle . . .

We're all allowed at least one frivolous item in our pack, and I am certainly no exception. On long (more than five-day) trips, I often carry along a pocket hammock. I got mine years ago, at the now defunct Camp & Trails outfitters in New York City. It's called a pocket hammock, but you'd need rather large pockets to house this item. The webbing is made from nylon cord, and it has a nylon line at each end. It can be quickly tied between two trees, where you can swing in the breeze and contemplate how beautiful it is to be here swinging in the breeze. I am told that hammocks of this type are widely used by climbers—held up, I would guess, in the absence of trees, by pitons and carabiners.

There are other gadgets and accessories, to be sure, and more are added to the shelves and catalogs every season. Before you buy, think about how the new item can be of help to you. Is it, in fact, a better mousetrap or simply a waste of money? Sometimes, when I am looking over equipment, lightweight foods and accessories, I think about the old-timers—such as John Muir and Bob Marshall. These men would spend weeks in the real wilderness with only a sack of beans, some flour, a blanket and a frying pan. An accessory to them was a pair of shoes *with* soles.

Section II

7 The Conservative Backpacker

It's not surprising that backpackers are generally more concerned than the general public with environmental issues. What is surprising is that the practitioners of this gentle art can be so savagely vocal about any intrusions on "their" land. Since backpackers tend to be urban/suburbanites, rural folks are equally quick to object to the environmentally predicated strictures that they, the year-round residents, feel threaten their livelihoods, lifestyles and the use of their land. The result has often been war when a mediated settlement would clearly be more productive.

A major source of confusion here is that these groups tend to define the very term "conservation" in different ways. According to the Oxford English Dictionary, there are at least two useful definitions. The first: "the action of conserving; preservation from destructive influences, natural decay or waste . . ." seems to support the position taken by rural folk who are really talking about "good husbandry" or maximal use without permanant damage. Sustained yield forestry would be one example of this type of approach.

The second definition, "preservation of existing conditions, institutions, etc." is closer to the way most backpacking and conservation groups view the situation.

In order to choose the direction of future change, examine first the concept of wilderness as spiritually uplifting or renewing. This is a relatively new concept; when you're struggling to make a living on the land, forests are seen as lumber and deer and other wildlife are looked upon as a threat to crops and herds.

The basis for the "spirituality" of the wilderness can be traced back to Rousseau and the romantics who built a mystique on his precept that "man is naturally good and only corrupted by civilization." If you accept this, then it follows that one can regain some portion of this "natural goodness" by returning to the wilderness. Thoreau helped spread this concept to America. Jefferson, too, in the drafting of the Constitution relied heavily on the rights of "natural" man in justifying a rebellion.

Conservation in America actually started as an elitist concept in the East as private citizens bought up large tracts of land for hunting and fishing clubs. The common man was excluded; he didn't have the time for leisure.

This tradition moved west and manifested itself in the founding of the Sierra Club, still one of the single most important conservation organizations in the country. Warren Olney, a lawyer, and David Star Jordan, President of Stanford University, got together with John Muir and others with the intention of both exploring and protecting the Sierra Nevada. Muir's position is usually misrepresented. He's seen as a bucolic sheepherder reformed by contact with the natural beauties of the Sierras. He did herd sheep in his salad days, but anyone who's visited his mansion in Martinez, California, can clearly see him as a more than prosperous "orchardist" whose profession allowed him to wander freely in the mountains in the summer.

The governmental agencies that were charged with holding the vast federal reserves of land virtually gave away much of the land to

John Muir, who helped launch The Sierra Club in 1892, was one of the pioneers in the conservation movement.

lumbermen, ranchers and miners. While the U.S. Commission of Fish and Fisheries was established in 1871, and the Forest Bureau in 1891, there was no public pressure for preserving our wilderness and scenic heritage.

Muir, Gifford Pinchot and others were writing and lecturing in an attempt to save what they could. It was Muir who, over a campfire in the Tuolumne Meadows area, persuaded *Century* Magazine editor Robert Underwood Johnson that Yosemite should be made a national trust. Johnson, well-connected in Congress, slipped the bill through before opposition could be mustered.

Yosemite had been a badly mismanaged California park since 1864; extensive sheep grazing and other reckless exploitations had damaged its meadows. It's ironic that Muir, the ex-sheepherder, was now the driving force for putting them under federal protection.

About this time, Teddy Roosevelt entered the conservation wars. He had entered Harvard with the intent of becoming a naturalist. His marriage to Alice Lee probably moved him away from this aim—he insisted it was Harvard's lab oriented approach that turned him off—but on her death, and that of his mother in 1884, he moved to the badlands of North Dakota and a ranching career. After San Juan Hill, he moved rapidly uphill in politics and became the 26th President when McKinley was assassinated in 1901.

He initiated the immense conservation program that resulted in bringing most of the best available lands under federal control. His support of farmers added at least three million acres to the American food base, and he added 150 million acres to national forests. He increased the number of national parks from five to ten, the number of wildlife refuges from 1 to 51, and he changed the shape of America's vacation habits by making camping and wilderness outings respectable. On the other hand, he was also an absolutely dedicated collector of dead animals—and a fine taxidermist—who shot anything that walked or flew.

Roosevelt saw wilderness as a testing place where Americans could grow fighting fit. The wilderness as challenge is still a fundamental part of many people's outdoor ethic.

Roosevelt's programs were brought to a halt by World War I; during this period, exploitation was the rule. By the twenties America was rolling. The combination of decent roads, a shorter

The Jeffrey Pine on Sentinel Dome, part of Yosemite National Park, which owes its existence to men like Muir. *(U. S. Department of the Interior, National Park Service photograph by Jean Speiser)*

work week and Roosevelt's example introduced more people to the wilderness than ever before.

The thirties brought camping to the fore as involuntary idleness made this inexpensive alternative to traditional resorts attractive. Kings Canyon National Park, the Jackson Hole area and others were added to the National Park System; after a fallow period during World War II, the rush to the forests and parks was on. Better roads, more cars and the awareness of natural wonders that the transplanted Easterner brought to the West led to a huge use increase.

Connecting links of the Applachian Trail, the establishment of the

83

Pacific Crest Trail and an expansion of state scenic rivers and park systems marked the next two decades. In California, a major effort was made to increase the size of redwood parks and to expand the protection offered existing parks to complete watersheds.

An important factor, which continues to influence the acquisition of lands, has been the cooperation of state and federal agencies and the willingness of the military to return parts of their land holdings to the people for recreational use. One unfortunate result of this acquisition period has been a dilution of available personnel. This has resulted in a deterioration of services.

The political, educational and personal efforts by *every* backpacker would no doubt improve the sport for all of us. A good first step would be to join a large organization where your membership fee would help support the conservation lobby at state and federal levels.

The Sierra Club, 530 Bush Street, San Francisco, CA 94108, with over 160,000 members, is probably the best known group of this kind. The Sierra Club has maximum clout politically, and there are fringe benefits that justify the membership fee. The monthly *Sierra Club Bulletin* and the annual *Ascent* are two.

The Wilderness Society, 1901 Pennsylvania Ave. NW, Washington DC 20006, serves as a coordinating body for local groups; its quarterly, *The Living Wilderness,* alone is worth the regular membership fee.

If you're interested in how your elected representatives voted on conservation matters you might consider checking with the League of Conservation Voters, 324 C Street SE, Washington, DC 20003; two biennials list the voting records of congressmen and senators respectively.

Other groups with political clout would include: The National Wildlife Federation, National Environmental Development Association, Natural Resources Defense Council, Environmental Defense Fund, Institute for Environmental Awareness, John Muir Institute for Environmental Studies and others.

In addition to membership in one or more of the above organizations, you will radically increase your backpacking skills and pleasures if you join a regional group. The advantage of state or even local groups is that you can focus on specific problems where an individual or group can make a direct contribution. Disgusted about the litter on your favorite trail? Organize a local group and clean it up yourself. Disturbed by the decline in trail maintenance locally? Get out your own shovel. Or you can combine this kind of citizen's self-help with a campaign in local papers to embarrass the neglectful parties.

It is extraordinary how much a few people can get done on a weekend it they're willing to work. Take a trip out before Memorial Day to spruce up local trails and a second trip after Labor Day to pick up litter. State and local rangers, foresters and even logging companies are usually willing to provide skilled direction and pickup of the litter you've bagged. Two weekends a year seems a reasonable price to pay for clean, well-maintained trails year-round.

You'll soon find you can get very hard-nosed about careless backpackers who drop things on "your" trail. If you take a more temperate approach, you can also serve as a teacher to the growing number of beginners who aren't familiar with proper trail etiquette.

Education is a sadly neglected part of the complete backpacker/ conservationist's skills. Whether it's introducing Scouts to the backcountry, or just offering casual suggestions in camp or on the trail to those who need help, you should always accept this responsibility. It's an important bit of your wilderness heritage, and skills not passed on are lost forever.

You've got to clean up your own act first. Old-fashioned systems of burning and then burying garbage have been replaced with a "take nothing but pictures, leave nothing but footprints" ethic. Wood has to be left on the ground where it belongs, not used to make ugly burn scars on granite that will remain forever. All waste must be packed out, or in the case of human waste, disposed of well away from camp.

Do not camp within a couple of hundred feet of water—running or still. You'll have to carry water to camp, but if your site is well above the water surface, you'll avoid most of the mosquitoes and other unpleasant vampires.

Stay on switchbacks rather than cutting across. Shortcutting switchbacks is a major cause of trail erosion in many areas of the country. If you notice small gully formations on these sections of trail, invest a moment and dump a couple of rocks into the canyon.

Do not take additional paths across meadows, particularly high country meadows. Restore multiple fire pits so you only leave one, or better none. Carry a trash pack when you're on short hikes so you can carry out what your predecessors left.

The most important step you may take to improve the quality of recreation in many areas is to stay away. Crowding on sections of the Appalachian and John Muir trails is unbelievable. Better hiking can now be found in many other less crowded areas. Consider famous trails or destinations of this type, a "one-shot" deal; limit yourself to a trip of this kind every ten years or so. To do otherwise is to deny the new backpacker the chance at something special, which you once had. So get out your topographic maps and look for other trails.The alternative is the deterioration of backcountry use for *all*.

CONSERVATION

Here's a rundown of some other significant conservation organizations. For a more detailed list of these and other groups, write to the National Wildlife Federation, 1412 16th St. NW, Washington, DC 20036. The Directory costs $6 plus shipping.

Adirondack Mountain Club, 172 Ridge St., Glens Falls, NY 12801; 8,000 members; chartered in 1922; publication: *Adirondac*.

Alpine Club of Canada, P.O. Box 1026, Banff, Alberta T0L 0C0, Canada; 2,800 members; founded in 1906; mountaineering group; annual publication: *Canadian Alpine Journal*; bi-annual *Gazette*.

American Hiking Society, 1701 18th St. NW, Washington, DC 20009; nonprofit organization created to provide and protect the interests of hikers; publications: *American Hiker, The Wilderness Bookstore Catalog, Trail Information Packets*.

Appalachian Mountain Club, 5 Joy St., Boston, MA 02108; 25,000 members; founded in 1876; maintains hut and shelter complex in New Hampshire's White Mountains; publications: *Appalachia, Appalachia Bulletin, AMC Guidebooks*.

Appalachian Trail Conference, P.O. Box 236, Harpers Ferry, WV 25425; 18,000 members; organized in 1925; maintains and preserves the 2,100-mile footpath; publications: *Appalachian Trailways News, The Register* (newsletter).

Colorado Mountain Club, 2530 W. Alameda Ave., Denver, CO 80219; 6,681 members; founded in 1912; collects and disseminates information on the Rocky Mountains; publication: *Trail and Timberline.*

Green Mountain Club, P.O. Box 889, 43 State St., Montpelier, VT 05602; 4,200 members; founded in 1910; maintains and protects the 430-mile Long Trail system; publication: *The Long Trail News.*

International Backpacker's Association, P.O. Box 85, Lincoln Center, ME 04458; 21,000 members; organized in 1973; maintains and protects trails and wilderness areas.

The Mountaineers, 719 Pike St., Seattle, WA 98101; 12,000 members; organized in 1906; explores, studies and preserves the Northwest wilderness.

National Audubon Society, 950 Third Ave., New York, NY 10022; 450,000 members; founded in 1905; maintains 76 sanctuaries and ten regional offices in addition to its Washington, DC office; provides research and nature centers, ecology camps, films and lectures; has more than 460 chapters; publications: *Audubon, Audubon Leader, American Birds.*

North America Trail Complex, P.O. Box 1805, Bloomington, IN 47402; founded in 1971; an ecocultural group whose aim is to establish a nationwide network of interconnecting footpaths; publication: *Wilderness Pocket Survival Cards.*

Potomac Appalachian Trail Club, 1718 N St. NW, Washington, DC 20036; 3,100 members; founded in 1927; maintains an 800-mile network of trails; mountaineering and ski-touring interests; publication: *Potomac Appalachian* (monthly).

Take training hikes with an overload. *(Mark J. Boesch)*

8 Physical Conditioning

The truth is that if you're in reasonable shape —and your load isn't too great—you can slap on a pack and slog any reasonable distance. The catch is that Americans as a group are in miserable physical condition. It is clear that our very low life span—for a developed country—is due not to problems of health care but to a combination of overeating and underexercising. The solution then, is not to get in shape for *backpacking* but to get in shape to extend your active life span. As a fellow outdoor writer succinctly put it, "Hell, I'm not getting older; I'm just getting fatter."

The basis for this leaner type of lifestyle is actually twofold: cardio-vascular fitness and weight control. From the Royal Canadian Air Force exercise book to rope skipping, you can find one thing in common with all systems. You've got to work *at least* every other day.

Reading this isn't going to get you up off your behind. Actually there is nothing anyone else can do for you. You're given your hereditary basics, and until about age 30 you can violate good sense; but after 30 you've got to earn the way you look and feel. Fun diets, instant exercise plans and the like are fraudulent and short term at best.

"Getting in shape" isn't just dropping weight and building muscles. Strength can be a factor in carrying heavy loads, but with modern backpacking gear, you'll rarely have to tote more than 25 percent of your body weight. Your first question should be, "What am I really trying to get in shape for?" The answer can be anything from being able to slowly chug three or four miles off the roadhead to running the Boston Marathon; your fitness program should reflect your needs.

The first thing most of us should do is take off all our clothes and stand in front of a full-length mirror. Several friends who are fighting the fatty demons say that looking at themselves naked in a full-length mirror every morning is all they need to do to keep on the gastronomic straight and narrow. At the same time you can also have a physical to see that you've nothing wrong with your body *before* you start an exercise plan. Don't, as so many do, start do-it-yourself systems without a checkup; all you'll do is overload your legs and you'll end up sitting more than walking.

Overload is, however, basic for exercise programs. All athletes train by moving longer, further or harder than their previous workout. But this overload is a gradual one that slowly builds up strength and endurance, not a destructive one that tears you down.

In order to establish a program you must first establish a base. One way of doing this is to see how long it takes for you to run a half mile or walk two miles. Your basic time—some will be *very* basic—will give you a standard against which you can measure improvement. Incidentally, you can often find high school or college coaches who are willing to help you with a training program. This type of *individual* professional training advice is probably the best. It will also make sure you get out on those days when you're feeling a bit lazy about training.

If you're on your own, or live in an area where it's difficult or unsafe to train after work, you might try one of the at-home systems. The Royal Canadian Air Force Exercise program is well-recommended. You can skip rope, *if* you also add other sports that will provide additional movement. Tennis, badminton, volleyball or basketball are good ways to get moving. Cold weather types can try squash, handball or cross-country skiing during the period when most people are only getting out of their chairs to change channels.

If you don't already participate in a sport on a regular basis, you should consider cycling, jogging or swimming as good "total" sports with strength elements that have a direct relationship to backpacking, with a heavy emphasis on cardio-vascular fitness. Cycling has specific advantages if you've a history of knee or ankle problems. Cycling is also a good *family* fitness sport; you can devise a handicap system using the high gears up hills so everybody arrives at the destination at the same time.

But even if you don't have the time—or won't make the time—for a fitness program, you can still make adjustments to your daily pattern that will help you on the trail. You can get off the bus a few stops before the usual one; you can walk up, or down, stairs instead of riding the elevator; and you can use your lunch break to window shop after a quick, light lunch instead of eating at a restaurant every day. You'll save enough on lunches to buy that Gore-Tex parka or expensive sleeping bag you've been lusting after.

Once you've spent a month or two in a general fitness program you can start with specific activities that are aimed at your backpacking needs. Backpacking is basically an endurance sport, but building stamina takes time. You should be careful in your exercise program to include both "interval sports"—like tennis where you operate at a maximum and then recover while chasing down balls—and endurance activities, where you maintain a more even output of energy. Sedentary sports like golf and bowling (and sex) don't count here.

Since the best way to train for a specific activity once you're reasonably fit is with an overload, your initial effort should be walking steep trails or sidewalks with a heavy weight in the pack you normally use. This is also a good way to break in your new boots. The hike should be at least as long as your normal day's backpacking trip. Realize that most backpackers only walk six or seven miles each way on a weekend trip; that's why only this length of training effort is needed. Once you've reached this level of fitness you can

91

easily handle a two-week seasonal trip as long as you start slowly and don't break down on the first day.

After you've chosen a route—uphill first and downhill back to your starting point mixed with a rolling middle section—you should walk the course at a brisk pace *without* a pack. Don't run. Just motor along at a rate that will keep your pulse pumping at a good working rate—about 120 beats a minute. If you get very tired, slow down; if you get chest pains, stop. When you get to the end of your hike, record your time. Your next step should be to add a pack and about five percent of your body weight in load.

Walk the course again while keeping tabs on your heartbeat. Once you can do the course under load with only mild discomfort, add another five percent to your pack. An easy way to vary your load here is to use plastic gallon containers that you can fill with water and weigh on the bathroom scales at home.

By hiking this course three or four times a week—five or six miles should take no more than two hours—you'll soon be able to carry loads up to 25 percent of your body weight. At this point you'll be quite fit enough for weekending.

Additional effort to make your trail loads seem lighter can involve weights up to 30 or 35 percent of your body weight. And if you can arrange it so you pack your course *before* dinner, you'll find that you'll be too tired to eat as much as you normally do. Actually, just not eating after five p.m. will take some weight off. The problem is that most people eat their big meal at dinner and then build fat while they watch the tube. A big breakfast, a light lunch and small dinner is a preferable system since your daily exercise program should burn off what you eat.

On the days when you're not hiking or doing other endurance training, you should concentrate on interval training to reduce your recovery time after periods of near-maximum stress. The experienced hiker has the ability to recover fast as well as the awareness of body needs that keeps him going only at the maximum for sustained effort. Beginners tend to lack this basic awareness and overload; then they collapse in a heap and lose all the time they gained by their super effort. Tortoises, not rabbits, should provide the pattern for the backpacker.

You'll note that up to this point *strength* has not been discussed.

The reason is simple. Strength is what the dilettante uses as a substitute for technique on the trail, and bulging muscles are no sign of real fitness for backpacking.

Most any program that brings you up to a reasonable level of fitness will build all the strength you'll ever need on the trail. You'll never have to move more weight than the amount your legs are already carrying.

ON THE TRAIL

Actual trail practice of your "pre-conditioning" can be divided into three parts: routing, pacing and trail techniques.

Routing is the best way to foul up a backpacking trip. Simply walking too far in a day—especially the first day when your pack is at its heaviest and your feet most tender—is guaranteed to cramp more than your style.

Six or seven miles is a good standard for a first day if you'd normally hike ten. Weekend hikes should also be scaled down from maximum distances; you'll be expending much energy during the day that won't show up on your total trail distance. You *can* discover quite isolated destinations just three or four miles from the road. A little research of topographic maps is essential.

Those strange little lines on the topo map indicate the price you must pay in chugging uphill. A good basis rule here is that one mile of distance is equal to 1,000 feet of uphill. A three-mile hike that rises 3,000 feet is equal, or greater, to a six-mile hike at sea level. Early in the season, downed trees or snowbanks can also increase your effort.

Pacing is only learned if you're attentive to the little signs of your body that come when you're asking too much of it. Experienced hikers don't walk much faster than beginners, but they *hike* much faster because they keep moving so their body has the chance to adjust to working under load. If you move so fast that you overload your system before you catch your "second wind" you will spend so much time sitting that you'll never adjust to a good pace.

Just the effort of swinging your pack to the ground and then picking it up can undo the savings in energy you get from a short rest. You should formulate a resting regimen. If you must stop at all, brace your pack against a tree or rest it on a boulder. A more experienced hiker stops on the trail for a short rest once every hour or so. Rest stops, especially if longer than three or five minutes, permit your body to "tune down"; then you've got to get things going from scratch every time you start out. This is just a waste of energy.

Fighting the weather more than you have to is wasteful, too. If your routing is right you should be able to hike only in the cool of the morning so you don't get cooked by the midday sun. Routing and pacing should overlap; you should adjust your route so you hike all switchbacks at a time when the sun is either still coming up or just going down. Best of all is getting up at first light and getting all your hiking in by ten or 11; then you can set up camp, fish and take pictures all afternoon.

Pace should be adjusted to meals as well. Don't move out at too brisk a pace after lunch. One solution to this is lots of nibbles all day instead of just a single heavy lunch.

Trail techniques are part of pacing, but these are limited to the actual way in which you hike. Since walking is a natural part of our lives, we all assume that we know how to hike. But hiking is a little more complex than sidewalk strolling. Certainly there are many stretches where you can amble along—open meadow trails or granite areas. But there are many more areas where attention to your prospective route in the next 20 or 30 yards is valuable. Even exact foot placement on a step by step basis will help reduce your efforts on many trails.

Now this may seem ludicrous to experienced hikers, but that's because they have the unconscious ability to take the easiest line and put each foot in the most advantageous spot. If you're a beginner, it is worthwhile to take the time to learn the right way to select a short-term route and individual foot spotting from the start.

Short-term route selection is based on the premise that, when hiking, the shortest distance between two points is rarely the straight line. To conserve the maximum amount of energy, it is much more useful to take a line that has a more gradual incline. Don't shortcut switchbacks, and you'll have made a start. Examine switchbacks more closely and you'll find that one side—usually the outside edge—is more gradually ascending than the other.

The thing that you're trying to avoid is vertical effort. Good hikers raise their boots just high enough to clear the ground, and downhills—especially if steep—are done in a kind of shuffle that flops boots down without any real muscular effort.

The experienced hiker uses a type of stride that's called "loose-kneed." He (or she) seems to glide along, never stepping up on a rock when it can be avoided, and there's a pause in the uphill stride that comes just when the person's weight passes over the load-bearing boot. The seasonal hiker also takes more steps than the beginner when going uphill and fewer steps on the level or downhill; the weight transfer from loaded to unloaded foot is smoother and much longer, with more hip movement.

The really proficient mountain man or woman has the self-confidence to admit that the projected hike is simply too much for that day. After a while, you'll find that you can adjust destinations, meal times and routes to achieve the maximum distance with the minimum amount of stress and discomfort.

Fitness for backpacking will increase your physical ability, mental toughness and technical skills off the trail as well.

On many trails, it's not uncommon to see hikers with long wooden packframes extending many feet above their heads. These particular contraptions are far from pedestrian, however.

9 Packing The Pack

Over the years I've collected just about all the backpack gear that I need for any trip I'm likely to take—from a weekend to a couple of weeks. My system for choosing what I'll want to take, and then packing it, is simple.

All my equipment—anything and everything I'm likely to need—is listed on a checklist. I even include such things as extra film for my camera and a pen for my shirt pocket (I never go anywhere without my pen). As I get a new piece of equipment, or think of something else I might someday need on the trail, down it goes on the list.

Needless to say, it's a long list. If I ever set out on a trip with everything, it would be quite a load—but then, I'd be carrying swimming trunks, bug repellent, snowshoes and ice creepers all at the same time. The point is that by having *everything* down on paper, it's easy to go down the list and check off the items I think I'll need. My list even includes a "Things To Do" section, including such things as trimming my toenails, waterproofing my boots and sharpening my pocket knife. There's also a separate list for "Food."

Let's assume that I'm planning an early-summer trip to the mountains for about five days to a week. Even in June it can get fairly chilly at night, so I'll want to be ready for evening temperatures as low as 30 degrees. During the day, I'm sure to be hot and sweaty—and insects may be a problem. If I have an idea of the weather conditions I'm most likely to run into, I should have a pretty good idea of what I'll be needing in the way of equipment.

First comes the pack itself. I have two packs. My first pack, which is still in good shape and serviceable, is a medium-sized canvas rucksack with leather straps connected to the bag by a sturdy brass ring. When I first started hiking, I would fill the sack with a down-and-feathers sleeping bag, a plastic canteen, a rain poncho, some food and very little else. That would hold me for anywhere from one night to three. Since then, I've developed a taste for some of the luxury items that add so much comfort to any backpack trip.

My second pack is an aluminum packframe with a large, undivided nylon bag. I like the big undivided bag—especially on those bitter winter mornings when you wake up in your tent and find that the temperature during the night has dropped down well below zero, and all you feel like doing is packing up fast and getting moving. Then it's nice to be able to throw everything into the bag—including your unrolled sleeping bag—and head out. Leather thongs tied to the zippers of the pack bag are also life savers for winter backpacking.

Anyway, first comes the pack. The general rule for loading a packframe is that the heaviest items go toward the top and as close to the frame as possible. In general this is impossible, and in an undivided pack bag it's even harder. Still, it's possible to get a fairly good approximation if you're careful.

The idea behind distributing the weight in this seemingly upside-down configuration is that with the weight up high and close to your back, the center of gravity of the pack is in a vertical line with your own center of gravity—or as close to it as possible. The farther "behind you" the pack's center of gravity is, the more you're pulled backward with each step and the more likely you are of losing your balance. The higher the center of gravity, the more the weight of the pack presses straight down on your shoulders, and the easier it is to carry. In New York's Adirondacks, it's not uncommon to see hikers with long wooden packframes extending many feet above their heads.

Another general consideration in packing, one that often conflicts with keeping the heavy items on top, is placing the equipment you may need in a hurry—such as a sweater, jacket or poncho—on top where you can get to it fast. As it happens, most of the really heavy pieces of equipment are the ones you don't need until you're ready to set up camp for the night: the ones you'd like to be able to bury somewhere near the bottom. It's here that the advantages of a divided bag shine.

At the very bottom of my bag goes the extra clothing and underwear. I will not give any advice on how much to bring. Some people insist on changing daily and some people hike *alone*. Remember that the weight of even the lightest items adds up, and the lighter the load the happier the hiker. Carrying too much can be a depressing experience.

Down there in the nether regions, amidst the underwear, also go such items as a towel and/or washcloth, extra shirt(s) and swimming trunks. For a five-day trip, I'd take one or two extra shirts. The swimming trunks don't get much use; I think I'll scratch them off my list for good.

Above the "linen closet," I like to put the food that I don't expect to use right away. Today's lunch goes right on top; tomorrow's lunch, tonight's dinner, etc., go on the bottom.

I repack most of the foodstuffs in plastic bags, each containing about one meal's worth. Then, I pack together—in larger bags—all the breakfasts, lunches, dinners and on-the-trail snacks.

The hardware goes above the pantry. Here I include: my 22-ounce Svea stove, which is well worth the effort in hauling it. For five-day trips, I would also take my one-pint aluminum gas bottle and a small plastic funnel (in an outside pocket). In here also goes a cylindrical candle lantern, which weighs next to nothing. If I think that I may be building a fire, for whatever reasons, I take along a folding saw. The model I have folds into its handle and locks into position with a wing-bolt at one end. Also available is a folding backpacker's saw that is triangular when extended and even lighter than mine. And then there's also a pocket saw, which merely consists of a flexible "chainsaw" with a ring at the end.

Still in the hardware section, I include a set of nesting pots (two). The larger of the two I use for preparing dehydrated meals, and the smaller for boiling water. When packing away the pots, I usually fill them with some of the foods I plan to cook in them. This not only saves precious space, but it protects the food from the sharp teeth of inquisitive rodents that may wander by at night. I do not take any additional plates.

If I am taking an air mattress (an admitted luxury), I first remove all air with the step pump, then fold the mattress and place it up against the back of the pack. The step pump goes in with the hardware. I prefer to use a lightweight Ensolite pad.

On top of all this I place a plastic bag containing a small bar of soap, razor, toothbrush and toothpaste, a small metal mirror and (sometimes) some baby powder.

Once all this is packed, I toss in today's lunch and a candy bar in a plastic bag; then I cover it all with a warm sweater and a rain poncho. Most everything else goes into pockets on the side of the pack: flashlight (with extra batteries and bulbs), maps and compass, toilet paper, insect repellent, matchbox (filled with my paraffin matches) and the first-aid kit.

I tie the sleeping bag and tent below (with the tent on bottom to protect the bag when pack is set on wet ground), the tent poles (if any) and mattress (if at all) above. That's it. It should weigh no more than 35 pounds, which is *about* one-quarter of my body weight. If it's much heavier than that, go down your checklist and get rid of the luxuries (swimming trunks, air mattresses, etc.).

Here's a backpacker's checklist that you might find handy. Feel free to rip it out of the book, sew it on your backpack, post it on the office bulletin board or drop it in a suggestion box.

But do remember a couple of things. The idea is not to take everything on the list, but to check the things you think you will be needing on one particular trip. What you will need is determined by where you are going, how long you plan to be staying, the expected weather conditions and where you plan on making camp.

- ☐ bus schedule (for towns along the route)
- ☐ camera (and film)
- ☐ candle holder (and candles)
- ☐ can opener
- ☐ canteen
- ☐ clothing (and underwear)
- ☐ compass
- ☐ cup
- ☐ first-aid kit
- ☐ flashlight (and batteries and bulbs)
- ☐ gaiters
- ☐ ground sheet
- ☐ handkerchief
- ☐ ice creepers
- ☐ insect repellent
- ☐ knife
- ☐ map
- ☐ match box (and matches)
- ☐ mattress and pump (or pad)
- ☐ memo book
- ☐ mittens
- ☐ needle and thread
- ☐ pen
- ☐ poncho
- ☐ pots and utensils
- ☐ powder (body)
- ☐ rope

- ☐ saw
- ☐ second pair of shoes
- ☐ shock cords (or straps)
- ☐ sleeping bag
- ☐ snowshoes
- ☐ soap
- ☐ steel wool
- ☐ stove (funnel and tank)
- ☐ sunglasses
- ☐ sweater
- ☐ swimming trunks
- ☐ tent
- ☐ tent pegs
- ☐ thermometer
- ☐ toilet paper
- ☐ towel
- ☐ wash cloth
- ☐ water bottle
- ☐ etc.

10 Hot-Weather Backpacking

"Summertime and the livin' is easy." That's what the song says. "But it ain't necessarily so." Gone are the icy winds of winter, the chilling dampness of snow camping and the ever-present threat of hypothermia. The warm sun feels good on your shoulders, and you don't have a care in the world as you start up the trail on a hot July day.

Four hours later, your 35-pound pack feels like 135 pounds. Your heart is pounding, your head is throbbing, your knees are weak and you feel like throwing up. It may be summertime, but the livin' isn't so easy anymore.

The human body is an extremely complex machine, designed to operate within a very narrow temperature range despite wide fluctuations in the environmental temperature. Fortunately, it is well equipped with a variety of heat conserving and dissipating mechanisms which make temperature control automatic in most situations. However, under extreme conditions, the body's thermal regulatory mechanisms cannot keep pace with the demands placed upon them, and trouble results. When the body loses heat faster than it is produced, the temperature falls, resulting in hypothermia. On the other hand, if the body is incapable of dissipating heat at a sufficient rate, its temperature rises, and a variety of heat-induced maladies can occur.

Ranging from mild nausea to the sometimes fatal "sun stroke," heat stress can be a very real threat to hot-weather backpackers. But, as with hypothermia, it can be quite easily avoided by those with proper knowledge.

While the body's control of heat loss and gain requires many subtle physiological adjustments, what's important to the backpacker are changes in blood flow and fluid balance. As the body temperature rises due to heavy work and a hot environment, blood vessels dilate and the heart rate increases to move blood from the hot interior to the cooler surface. Sweating begins in an attempt to increase the rate of evaporative cooling from the skin. If, however, evaporative cooling is insufficient, the load upon the circulatory system increases as the body makes a futile attempt to move more blood for cooling. Increased sweating, which ensues, leads to shifts in the body's fluid balance, internal dehydration and loss of body salts. Ultimately, circulatory "collapse" results, and the victim may suffer any one of several consequences.

It is apparent, then, that preventing severe heat stress is at least partially related to one's ability to maintain adequate evaporative cooling.

For every liter of sweat that evaporates from the skin, the body loses 580 kilocalories of heat. Under very severe heat stress, the body may lose up to about three liters of sweat per hour. This sweat rate cannot be maintained for long, however, and only a fraction of the sweat is available for cooling—that which actually evaporates. The sweat that drips from your brow, for example, plays no part in cooling but only contributes to the loss of body fluids and salts.

While body weight is approximately 70 percent water, only about two percent of this water is available for sweating. As this "sweat reservoir" is depleted, additional fluid is drawn from the body cells, producing internal dehydration. Along with the elevated rate of sweating and dehydration, the loss of body salts is greatly increased.

Such dehydration and salt loss can continue for only a short time before the sweating mechanism shuts down to conserve body water and salts. The cessation of sweating under the conditions of heavy work in a hot environment is a final warning that circulatory collapse is imminent. It must not be ignored.

Normally, in a sedentary individual, the body's fluid balance is regulated very precisely. On the average, we take in approximately 2,500 milliliters (ml.) of fluid per day through actual diet and oxidation. We lose a similar amount through the urine, solid wastes, breathing and perspiring. Our thirst mechanism and urinary output fluctuate to maintain this fluid balance. Under conditions of heavy work in the heat, however, this balance is disturbed due to the tremendous increase in water loss. Remember: up to 3,000 ml. of sweat per hour can be lost during severe conditions.

Research has shown that when individuals dehydrate to a six percent loss of body weight, they suffer a 37 to 44 percent loss of their working capacity. On the other hand, if the water lost as sweat is adequately replaced by drinking during the exposure to heat, there is no loss of working capacity.

It has also been demonstrated that increased water loss through sweating increases cardiovascular stress. Adequate water replacement during the working period prevents such an increase in heat rate and blood pressure.

The implication seems clear. In order to prevent the loss of working capacity due to excessive sweating and dehydration, *adequate water must be consumed during the work period.* Unfortunately, many individuals, particularly athletes, have been led to believe that it is a cardinal sin to drink water during heavy exercise. I can still hear my coach imploring us, "Don't drink it. Just rinse your mouth and spit it out." It's a wonder we all didn't collapse.

Under severe heat stress, the normal thirst mechanism is inadequate to insure complete replacement of the water lost as sweat. Therefore, it is necessary to drink more water than you may feel you need. This is best accomplished by drinking small amounts at short intervals rather than by gulping down an enormous quantity during a single rest stop.

It has become my habit when backpacking in hot weather never to cross a stream or other source of potable water without taking a few sips and urging my companions to do the same. When such water is scarce, I make it a point to drink from my canteen at regular intervals. It goes without saying that *every* member of a group should carry a canteen, keep it filled and use it often. *The most important rule in the prevention of heat stress is to drink plenty of fluids.*

Replacing lost water is only part of the battle against heat stress. As mentioned earlier, when the body loses sweat, salts are also lost. This causes a further shift in the fluid balance. If certain types of heat stress are to be avoided, these salts must be replaced along with the water. Simply replacing the water is not enough.

Several methods exist for replacing lost body salts. However, for the backpacker, most of them have several drawbacks. A number of "hot weather" drinks are commercially available. These are chemically balanced to be almost identical in composition to body fluids. Such drinks are often used by athletes, and they are quite effective. Unfortunately, their bulk and relatively high cost often preclude their use by backpackers.

Another practice is to take salt tablets. While such tablets are both convenient to carry and use, they can lead to additional problems. When taken in such concentrated form, the elevated salt content of the stomach can cause nausea and irritation of the stomach lining and small intestine. It may cause vomiting and, thus, further dehydration.

The increased salt content of the stomach causes a shift of body fluids into that organ at the expense of other body tissues. This further increases internal dehydration. Either way, problems result. If you feel you must take salt in tablet form, it is imperative to drink an adequate amount of water. Preferably, take the tablets at mealtime.

Many exercise physiologists feel that it is best to avoid salt in tablet form under all but the most severe conditions of heat stress. In all other cases, adequate replacement of body salts can be accomplished by simply salting food a little more than usual. The latter method is much more palatable and does not cause the problems associated with salt tablets. Fortunately for the backpacker, many commercially-dehydrated foods are naturally quite salty.

The alert backpacker can also avoid problems with heat stress by learning to recognize the conditions during which it is most likely to occur. Since the body's major defense against overheating is evaporative cooling, anything which interferes with this process increases the probability of heat stress.

Contrary to popular opinion, air temperature is a relatively poor indicator of heat stress potential since it gives little information concerning the environmental capacity for evaporative cooling. A much better indication of possible heat stress is found in the relative humidity, which measures the amount of moisture in the air compared with the amount of water it could hold at that temperature if completely saturated.

Dry air—that is, air with a low relative humidity—permits rapid evaporation of sweat and a high rate of evaporative cooling even at high environmental temperatures. On the other hand, with high relative humidity, the rate of evaporation is sharply decreased along with the cooling potential.

The difference in relative humidity explains why a hiker in the West may feel quite comfortable with the temperature in the 90s whereas an eastern hiker may feel great discomfort. In the dry western air the hiker may not even notice that he is sweating due to the rapid rate of evaporation, while in the humid eastern air the hiker may be drenched with sweat. It should be noted, however, that the hiker in dry air is still losing a great deal of moisture and must still replace the fluids by drinking plenty of water.

A simple device called a sling psychrometer can be constructed to aid in estimating the threat of heat stress due to relative humidity. The apparatus consists of a thermometer mounted on a board which is attached at one end to a handle that permits the board to swing freely. The bulb of the thermometer is encased in a piece of light cotton cloth which is saturated with water and allowed to equilibrate with the air temperature. The device is then rotated vigorously by the handle, and the moisture evaporates from the cloth, reducing the temperature of the thermometer. This "wet bulb temperature" is an excellent indicator of the potential heat stress of the environment.

Three major problems can occur as a result of excessive heat stress: muscle cramps, heat exhaustion and heat stroke, often called "sun stroke." Of the three, muscle cramps are probably the most common—and also the easiest to prevent and treat. For the backpacker, such cramps usually occur in the legs and lower back and are the result of excessive water and salt loss due to sweating. Rest periods which allow the body to cool will usually relieve the cramps at least temporarily; a gentle massage may be of some help. It makes more sense, however, to prevent cramps altogether by drinking adequate water and taking care to increase your intake of salt when hiking in the heat. The likelihood of getting muscle cramps is also reduced as the hiker becomes acclimatized to hot weather backpacking.

Heat exhaustion—a more serious condition—can strike the unwary hiker quite suddenly and with little warning. It is the result of blood rushing to the vessels of the skin for cooling at the expense of blood flow to the brain and other organs. Heat exhaustion usually occurs following several hours of strenuous work in a hot environment and causes a rapid or irregular pulse rate, nausea, profuse sweating and a feeling of lightheadedness. The victim may faint, and his skin will be pale and cool. His body temperature will be near normal. It is extremely important to recognize these signs as distinct from the symptoms of heat stroke. The treatment for each condition is quite different.

The victim should lie down in the shade with his feet slightly elevated, and any tight clothing should be loosened to aid the circulation. He should be given cool, slightly salted drinks unless vomiting occurs; then, the liquids should be discontinued. Normally, administer half a glass of water containing half a teaspoon of salt every 15 minutes. The victim will usually recover after 30 to 60 minutes. If the pulse rate has slowed to under 90 beats per minute and the sweating has stopped, he can continue hiking at a reduced pace. He should be encouraged to eat high energy snacks along the trail, and increase his intake of both water and salt.

Heat stroke (sun stroke) is by far the most serious of the three heat-induced dangers and presents a real medical emergency. In heat stroke, the sweating will have stopped, and the skin will be dry, hot and red. The pulse will be rapid and strong, and the body temperature may be as high as 105 degrees F. The victim may suffer a loss of coordination, be confused or lose consciousness.

Once the above signs appear, the treatment must be immediate. The victim must be rapidly cooled by any means possible. He should be placed in the shade with most of his clothing removed and should be completely immersed in the cool water of a lake or stream. If this cannot be done, he should be covered with soaking wet clothing or at least swabbed with cool water or alcohol. Fanning the victim with towels or clothing will increase the evaporative cooling, and massaging the extremities will help to circulate the cooled blood to the hot interior of the body.

The victim should not be allowed to continue hiking even after an apparent recovery but should be evacuated for medical treatment. During the evacuation, he should be observed closely for a sudden rise in temperature or a relapse. Never underestimate the seriousness of an episode of heat stroke.

While the physiological mechanisms are not well understood, it is possible to acclimatize to working in a hot environment. The acclimatized individual is able to work at a lower body temperature, with lower blood pressure and heart rate, reduced metabolic cost and a more normal blood flow distribution between the skin and working muscles. At the same time, his sweat production increases by as much as 100 percent for better evaporative cooling. The sweat is more diluted, so body salts are conserved.

Acclimatization begins with the first exposure to heat, progresses very rapidly and is usually complete within four to seven days, but the method of becoming acclimatized is quite specific. Simple sedentary exposure to a hot environment does not produce acclimatization. Rather, one should participate in short intermittent periods of exercise, such as a couple of one-hour workouts each day in the heat. Workouts should be made progressively longer and more difficult, and maximum work should not be attempted before the acclimatization is complete. If maximum work is performed too soon, the acclimatization process will be delayed.

While a high level of physical fitness does not automatically produce acclimatization, a physically-fit individual will generally acclimatize more rapidly than one who is unfit. It has also been found that acclimatization to a hot, dry environment will improve performance in a hot, wet environment as well and vice-versa. Obviously acclimatization to severe conditions will facilitate performance under less severe conditions.

It is very important to drink plenty of water and take steps to replace lost body salts during the acclimatization process or the time required for acclimatization may be increased considerably. It should also be noted that an acclimatized individual will still be required to drink a great deal of water while hiking, since he or she will actually be sweating more. There is no way to train an individual to require less water under conditions of high environmental heat.

Once acclimatization has been achieved, it will be retained for approximately two weeks with no further exposure to a hot environment; most of it will be lost within two months. If a high level of physical fitness is maintained, the acclimatization will be retained somewhat better. If you desire to retain complete acclimatization, periodic work in the heat is required at intervals of no more than two weeks.

If a few simple precautions are taken, the problems inherent in hot weather backpacking can be reduced to a minimum. Wear a wide-brimmed hat to shade your head and light, loose clothing to permit air movement next to your skin. Wear sunglasses and a protective sun screen. If at all possible, try to become acclimatized before undertaking major trips in hot weather. While on the trail, salt your food a little more heavily than usual and rest often. Above all, *drink plenty of water,* and the livin' should be easy.

11 Cold-Weather Backpacking: I

WINTER HIKING

The two major differences between winter and summer hiking are cold weather and the likelihood of snow on the ground. Take away the squadrons of mosquitoes and black flies. Dismiss the throngs of summer backpackers. Keep a cool head; guard against cold feet, and you're there.

Winter backpacking is not an activity that is accessible to all warm-weather hikers. But, by and large, it is the same pursuit—only with increased amounts of common sense. As well as more preparation, more equipment, more clothes, more food and more caution. The one true and ubiquitous danger is that of hypothermia, which is as threatening in warm weather when temperatures precipitously drop. A comprehensive discussion on hypothermia follows this section.

111

Plan your winter trek with these four basics in mind: current and predicted temperatures; accumulated snow on the ground and the chances of more to come; what month of the year; possibility of an avalanche.

If wintertime temperatures have been hovering around the 30-degree mark, gear yourself and your camp for temperatures at that range and lower. Do not trust predicted forecasts that promise a warming trend.

For all practical purposes, the average hiker can be comfortable in a winter temperature range between 10 and 40 degrees. Warmer temperatures, of course, are fine. But temperatures that dip below ten degrees, and stay there for an extended period of time, can be uncomfortable. Wind is also an important consideration since it can increase the chill factor.

The amount of snow on the ground could affect your access into a particular area. You might consider using snowshoes, which are easier to handle than skis and offer more stability when you have a heavy pack on your back.

Heavy, wind-blown snow is a serious factor to consider. Familiar trails can be unrecognizable. Popular landmarks may be disguised. Whiteouts—gray-white sky plus falling snow on already snow-covered terrain—are particularly perilous. Do not travel during whiteouts.

Heavy snowfall can usually be accurately predicted. It is best not to plan a trip when winter storms are virtually certain to strike. Try to choose a stable weather period.

January and February are usually the coldest months of the year. In most areas of the country, backpackers can expect the severest cold-weather test during these months. March is the most erratic weather month of the year; high winds, wet snowfalls and stinging cold is usually the norm.

April through mid-May still qualify as winter camping months in most northern latitudes. These months usually afford good opportunities to espy wildlife. With the ice melting off many lakes and ponds, the fishing is excellent.

Avalanches are another great danger. Steep, narrow canyons are particularly vulnerable to avalanches early in winter when snow is

Snowshoes are easier to handle than skis and offer more stability when you have a pack on your back. *(Linda Curtis)*

113

neither settled nor packed. Avoid such areas, and check with the Forest Service or National Park Service personnel for a specific list of avalanche-prone areas.

For snow camping, the fly is usually anchored by a heavy object such as a rock.

(Carroll Seghers II)

There are tents especially designed for mountain or cold weather camping. Most of them are rather small and have few, if any, zippered windows. The entryway is narrow, often tunnel-like, to discourage gusts of cold air from entering. The smaller the tent, the more effective body heat is as a warming agent. Heat sources, such as catalytic stoves or compact wood-burning units known as sheepherder stoves, are more efficient in small, winter tents. Special attention is paid to adequate and safe ventilation for the heat source.

The small mountain tents are usually made of nylon. The best ones have an exterior, aluminum frame that works on a spring or flexbar principle. This framework keeps the nylon taut. It frees the winter backpacker from the burden of guy ropes and stakes; some type of extra support is advisable to keep the tent in place when no one is in it. Such tents can usually be anchored by nylon rope from grommets to trees or with rock or tree stump "anchors."

An important addition to the winter tent is a fly. For mountain tents, the fly is usually made of nylon and covers the entire tent with an air space of two to five inches between the main walls and roof and the fly itself. For snow camping, the fly is usually anchored with long sticks, rocks or stumps.

Air space between fly and wall is a great winter insulator. In fact, most campers find the tent to be so airtight they need a bit of ventilation to prevent excessive, interior condensation. A zippered slit or sky hatch in the roof of the main tent is one way to regulate ventilation.

In extremely cold climates, I have known some winter back-packers who will use two tents—a smaller one inside a larger one—for the ultimate in insulation.

Another alternative is a catalytic heater, which runs on white gas or propane. You'll note most of these cozy suggestions add quite a bit to your load. It comes with the territory. As do extra-warm sleeping bags and winter hiking clothes.

There are many wool-nylon-goose down—or synthetic fill—"layer" formulas geared for winter use.

I use a pure, unprocessed, loose-fitting wool sweater as an undershirt. This kind of wool does not scratch or itch. For long johns, the fishnet weave does not trap moisture. Most fishnet pants are made of cotton. Wool is better, and some manufacturers of expedition gear are now producing them. Cotton absorbs moisture like a sponge; wool does not. Most cold and chilling on winter campouts comes from damp underclothing. Wool does not absorb perspiration; if there are adequate air spaces between the layers of clothing, moisture can dry up. With cotton, this process takes a long time and the drying period can be very uncomfortable.

Add a pair of medium or heavy weight wool pants over the fishnet. Most sporting goods stores and expedition mail-order houses carry good wool trousers. Buy them loose-fitting. Women can purchase men's small sizes. They won't do much for the figure but the pants will be warm and give you plenty of freedom of movement.

Medium weight wool shirts, with plenty of room, are more comfortable and less restrictive than one, heavy weight shirt. The lighter shirts can be shed or added according to body needs.

During physical activity—such as chopping wood, digging ice holes or ski touring—this is probably all the clothing that will be needed, except for a wool cap and woolen mittens or gloves. Possibly the addition of an uncoated, breathable nylon wind shirt or parka would be helpful in order to shield against the wind or help shed moisture.

After the physical activity, a coat of goose down or synthetic fill will keep a camper warm. When to shed and when to add layers of wool, nylon or goose down is the most important consideration for keeping warm and dry in the winter.

In addition to woolen gloves, mittens and caps, nylon shells made to fit them can be added to repel moisture and act as "windshields."

For the feet, wear two pairs of heavy woolen Ragg socks inside a pair of rather loose fitting rubber-bottomed, leather-topped pacs. I recommend pacs that are made to be worn with woolen felt liners; they can be removed for airing and drying when need be. Buy pacs with plenty of foot room so that they fit pretty loosely when worn with two pairs of wool socks. Tight-fitting boots cut off circulation, causing cold, damp feet. Cold feet, for many reasons, can ruin a winter hiking trip.

Other handy clothing items are gaiters—nylon leggings worn over pants and boots to keep out snow and shed moisture. Woolen face masks (ski masks) can really help in heavy wind conditions. During winter, the hardest parts of the body to keep warm are feet, hands and face. Winter clothing should be specialized enough for adequate protection.

Many of these weighty cold-weather considerations are just common sense; if you already have it in abundance, you could formulate your own list of winter tips. However, for those who readily admit to a paucity of common sense—or for those who wish to be doubly prepared—tape these ten tiny tips to the back of your pack.

1. Outside campfires may feel good and add psychological warmth but if they melt snow and ice on clothing, making clothes wet or damp, fires do more harm than good. When away from the fire, campers "feel" the cold more. If you need to get warm, use tent stove and dry clothing.

2. Brush off as much snow as possible from clothes before entering warm tent.

3. Hang clothing for airing and drying inside tent.

4. Do not sleep in wet or damp clothing, especially socks.

5. A woolen stocking cap helps retain body heat—good when sleeping.

6. Ventilate before getting too warm; avoid sweating; add clothes before getting too cold.

7. On side trips, pack extra clothes, snacks and matches in day pack and wear at all times.

8. Guard against frostbite by checking for "white spots" on nose, face, ears and feet. Wind-chill factor may increase chances of frostbite. Protect extremities with wool or nylon.

9. Drink plenty of hot chocolate and eat high calorie, high protein snacks.

10. Buy the best high-grade woolen clothing, goose down or synthetic fill garments you can afford.

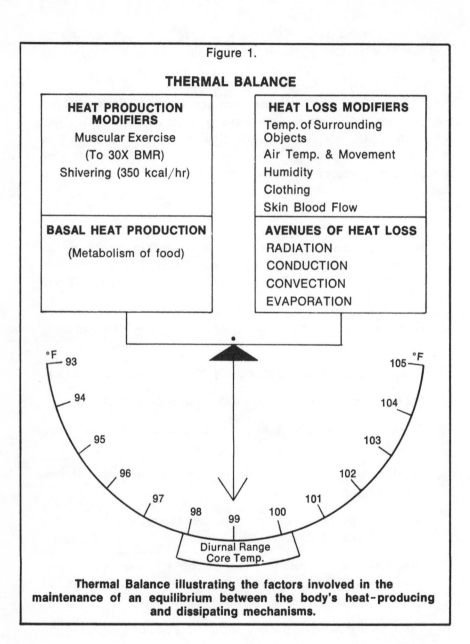

Figure 1.

THERMAL BALANCE

HEAT PRODUCTION MODIFIERS
Muscular Exercise
(To 30X BMR)
Shivering (350 kcal/hr)

HEAT LOSS MODIFIERS
Temp. of Surrounding Objects
Air Temp. & Movement
Humidity
Clothing
Skin Blood Flow

BASAL HEAT PRODUCTION
(Metabolism of food)

AVENUES OF HEAT LOSS
RADIATION
CONDUCTION
CONVECTION
EVAPORATION

°F 93 94 95 96 97 98 99 100 101 102 103 104 105 °F

Diurnal Range Core Temp.

Thermal Balance illustrating the factors involved in the maintenance of an equilibrium between the body's heat-producing and dissipating mechanisms.

12 Cold-Weather Backpacking:II

HYPOTHERMIA

Man, being a warm-blooded animal, must maintain a state of thermal balance. That is, he must produce and dissipate heat at a rate which will maintain his body temperature within a relatively narrow range. If the body fails to produce a sufficient amount of heat, or if heat is lost too rapidly, the body temperature will fall. This condition is the insidious hypothermia.

Hypothermia is responsible for an untold number of deaths each year. But the real tragedy is that the majority of these deaths could have been prevented if the victims had a basic knowledge of the body's mechanisms for producing and dissipating heat.

The primary source of the body's heat is the metabolism of the food that is eaten. Since the human body is only 20-30 percent efficient at best, only a relatively small proportion of food energy is converted to useful work. The remainder of the energy is the form of heat which is used to maintain the body temperature.

Two other factors can modify the body's heat production. As is obvious to anyone who has ever exercised sufficiently to work up a sweat, physical activity is an important source of heat and can increase the basal heat production by as much as 30 times. Shivering as a result of body cooling can produce as much as 350 kilocalories (kcal.) per hour.

Thus we have three methods of producing heat: we can eat, we can work and we can shiver.

If the body simply continued to produce heat, its temperature would rise by approximately three to four degrees Fahrenheit per hour at rest. Therefore, to maintain a relatively constant body temperature, heat must be dissipated as it is produced. As shown in Figure 1, there are four major avenues of heat loss along with a number of heat-loss modifiers. An understanding of these factors is essential if one is to cope with the threat of hypothermia.

Radiation may be defined as the exchange of heat energy between two objects not in contact with each other by means of electromagnetic waves. The net direction of heat loss will be from the warm object to the cooler one. Thus, we can gain heat by being close to a hot object such as a stove or a fire, or we can lose heat by radiation when we are in close proximity to large cold objects such as rocks and ice.

The rate at which heat is lost by radiation depends upon the temperature difference between the two objects, the surface area available for radiation, and the radiation coefficient of the warm object. The latter factor simply relates to an object's efficiency as a radiator. Human skin (of all colors) has a high radiation coefficient and is an excellent radiator.

Conduction is the transfer of heat energy between two objects that are touching each other, and the rate of heat loss depends upon the temperature difference, the area of contact and the conducting ability (i.e., conductance) of the materials. Materials with a low conductance are called insulators. Thus, even though the silver fork and the dinner napkin are both at identical temperatures, the fork will feel very cold to the skin since ·the metal has a higher conductance than the cloth and will drain heat away from the body at a faster rate. (The conductance of several important materials is shown in Table 1.)

Table 1.

Thermal conductance of various materials. A substance with a large thermal conductance transfers heat more rapidly than a substance with a low thermal conductance.

THERMAL CONDUCTANCE
(kcal/hr.m.^{2}Deg.C)

Still Air	2.3
Body Fat	14.4
Muscle	39.6
Water	53.0

Table 2.

WIND-CHILL*

Estimated Wind Speed (mph)	Air Temperature (°F)									
	50	40	30	20	10	0	—10	—20	—30	—40
	Equivalent Temperature (°F)									
CALM	50	40	30	20	10	0	—10	—20	—30	—40
5	48	37	27	16	6	—5	—15	—26	—36	—47
10	40	28	16	4	—9	—21	—33	—46	—58	—70
15	36	22	9	—5	—18	—36	—45	—58	—72	—85
20	32	18	4	—10	—25	—39	—53	—67	—82	—96
25	30	16	0	—15	—29	—44	—59	—74	—88	—104
30	28	13	—2	—18	—33	—48	—63	—79	—94	—109
35	27	11	—4	—20	—35	—49	—67	—83	—98	—113
40	26	10	—6	—21	—37	—53	—69	—85	—100	—116

Wind speeds greater than 40 mph have little additional effect	Little danger for properly clothed person	Increasing danger	Great danger
			DANGER OF FREEZING EXPOSED FLESH

*The Wind-Chill chart illustrates the influence of the wind upon heat loss. The values in the table are the effective temperature at a given air temperature (top row) and wind speed (left column).

Convection is the loss of heat as a result of the movement of the fluid medium (air or water) which surrounds the body. The body warms a thin layer of adjacent air by means of radiation, but, warm air being lighter than cold, this warm air rises and is replaced by cooler air which again must be heated. In this way, the body constantly loses heat by convection. Of course, if there is further air movement due to wind or the movement of the body through the medium, a greater amount of heat is lost. The accompanying "wind chill" chart (Table 2) illustrates the influence of the wind in producing "effective temperatures" which are far below the actual air temperature.

The rate of heat loss by convection is dependent upon the temperature difference between the body and the environment, the surface area which is exposed, and the amount of air (or water) movement.

Whenever an object changes state, i.e., goes from a solid to a liquid or from a liquid to a gas, heat is required. We add heat to convert ice (solid) to water, or to boil water and convert it to steam (gas). Ice in a drink melts and draws heat from the drink to cool it. In the same way, when moisture evaporates from the surface of the body when we leave the water after swimming, the heat required by the change of state is taken from the body and we feel cool even on a very warm day. Thus, *evaporation* is a fourth avenue of heat loss.

The human body is fighting a constant battle to maintain a state of thermal equilibrium. It must produce sufficient heat to maintain its temperature but must lose it rapidly enough to prevent overheating. At the same time, heat cannot be lost faster than it is produced. Normally, this process is automatically regulated very precisely, and we remain comfortable. For the backpacker, however, fighting this battle is not always so easy. If the battle is lost, hypothermia will be the victor, and death by "exposure" can be the result.

Contrary to popular opinion, extreme cold is not required to produce hypothermia. In fact, a person is probably less likely to experience the problem during very cold weather because he is better equipped to face the situation. The vast majority of deaths by hypothermia have occurred with the air temperature in the 32-55-degree range.

The conditions which are conducive to the development of hypothermia are quite predictable. They include fatigue, cool air temperature, wetness and wind. If several of these factors are present hypothermia is a real threat; if all four exist hypothermia is almost a certainty.

Hypothermia typically begins with a deterioration of the weather. The temperature falls or is already relatively cool, contributing to the body's loss of heat by radiation. If the potential victim is hatless, the loss of heat can be very significant. At rest as much as 50 percent of the body's heat production can be lost through radiation from the head and neck at an air temperature of 25 degrees.

As the victim's body begins to cool, its first line of defense will be to constrict the skin's blood vessels (vasoconstriction) in an attempt to shift the blood toward the body's core to prevent further heat loss. The blood flow to the fingers and toes may fall to one percent or less of normal. The blood vessels in the head and neck, however, do not respond in this manner, and the loss of heat through these areas continues unless the head is covered.

In an attempt to generate more heat and keep its core temperature within the 97-99-degree range, the body may begin to shiver. While shivering may increase the basal heat production by as much as five times, it cannot replace the heat already lost.

If the weather is rainy or the clothing is soaked from sweat or a stream crossing, the rate of heat loss is increased tremendously. As shown in Table 1, the thermal conductance of water is roughly 23 times that of dry air. Wet clothing loses its insulating value, and the water rapidly drains the heat away from the body. If the victim is lean and muscular, he has further difficulty retaining heat due to the high thermal conductance of muscle tissue.

By the time the wind comes up, the victim may be losing heat much faster than he can replace it even by vigorous exercise. With the increased wind comes an increased heat loss by both convection and evaporation.

Now the victim is becoming fatigued, and it is difficult for him to continue working; this further decreases his heat production. If he sits down to rest he loses still more heat through conduction to the ground, rock, or stump upon which he is sitting.

The situation has now become desperate. As the body's core

123

temperature falls to near 95 degrees, the heat producing mechanisms are actually inhibited, and the temperature drop becomes even more rapid. At a core temperature of 90-95 degrees, involuntary shivering becomes massive and violent. Such shivering is a danger sign that the body temperature is falling to the critical level. The victim will begin to lose his coordination and may stumble repeatedly. His speech may become slurred, and, as heat loss continues, he may become disoriented and even suffer from hallucinations. The mental confusion may well prevent the victim from taking protective measures even though he may have warm clothing and a dry sleeping bag in his pack. His physical condition may prevent him from striking a match or hooking a zipper.

The presence of *any* of the above signs indicate that the body is unable to cope with the loss of heat, and the situation requires *immediate and rapid treatment.* Hiking partners should continually be alert to these signs in each other any time environmental conditions indicate the danger of hypothermia.

If untreated at this point, the core temperature of the body continues to fall. At 86-91 degrees shivering may stop and the muscles become rigid. The loss of the shivering mechanism results in an even faster drop of the core temperature, and at 86-87 degrees the victim may become unconscious. At 80-85 degrees respiratory and/or cardiac arrest may occur. Death is almost certain with a core temperature of less than 80.

It is readily apparent that by the time many of the symptoms of hypothermia have developed, the body core temperature has already dropped significantly and the situation is quite critical. If the victim is to survive, treatment must be immediate. Many of the deaths due to hypothermia have occurred within one half to 1½ hours following the development of the first major symptoms.

Since the cause of hypothermia is a reduction in body heat production coupled with a profound loss of body heat, the treatment is aimed at the replacement of heat and the prevention of further loss. This treatment can be summarized in three steps: shelter the victim from the adverse weather conditions, remove his wet clothing and rewarm him as rapidly as possible.

In most field situations, adequate shelter will have to be improvised from materials at hand. If a tent is available, it should, of course, be used even if it can only be marginally erected. If no tent is available, ponchos, rain flys, clothing, canoes, tree boughs or many other materials can be utilized to construct emergency cover. Care should be taken to see that the shelter is protected as much as possible from both wind and moisture to reduce further cooling. For the same reason, the victim must be insulated from the ground upon which he is lying. Clothing, blankets and sleeping bags on top of the victim will do no good if his heat is being drained off from below.

While the shelter is being constructed, the victim's wet clothing should be removed completely and he should be dried off immediately. He should be placed into a *pre-warmed* sleeping bag as soon as possible. Under no circumstances should he be placed into a cold bag as this will merely compound the problem. The victim will be producing very little heat and it will be insufficient to warm the sleeping bag. The bag can be pre-warmed by another person or by well-wrapped heated rocks or canteens.

Ideally the best method of rapid rewarming is complete immersion in a hot bath (110-112 degrees). However, such facilities are rarely available in an emergency situation in the field. Thus, the rewarming must be done as efficiently as possible by other means. Skin-to-skin contact with another warm body provides an excellent method of rewarming, and a stripped companion should be placed in the sleeping bag with the victim. If a double bag is available and one person can be placed on each side of him so much the better.

If the victim is conscious and coherent, he should be given as much hot food and drink as possible both for the warmth and to give him an energy supply for producing heat by his own metabolism. Carbohydrates will provide more quick energy than either fats or proteins. Under no circumstances should alcoholic beverages be given. While these do provide a certain amount of quick energy and a feeling of warmth, they also cause a dilation of the blood vessels, and they are rapidly burned, ultimately leading to an increase in heat loss. If nothing else, hot water laced with sugar would be a better drink than alcohol.

During all phases of the rewarming procedure, it is imperative that the victim be watched closely for further deterioration and cardiac or respiratory arrest as a result of temperature "afterdrop."

As the rewarming begins, the skin's blood vessels will dilate, bringing blood to the surface. But, since this blood must first pass through chilled body tissue, it can actually become cooler and cause a further reduction in temperature when it returns to the body core. If the victim's core temperature is already near the critical level for survival, this "afterdrop" could prove fatal. The rescuer should be prepared to begin cardiac massage and artificial respiration at any time.

In fairly moderate cases of hypothermia, the victim should make no attempt to continue traveling until rewarming is complete, and he is dry, rested, and well fed. With more severe hypothermia, the victim should not be allowed to travel under his own power, but should be transported *in the horizontal position* if possible. Forced exercise during or immediately following rewarming may precipitate cardiac failure due to increased cardiac sensitivity and the effect of the cold on the general circulation. In all cases, medical attention should be sought as soon as possible.

While it is important for every outdoorsman to be familiar with the symptoms and treatment of hypothermia, it is even more essential to know how to prevent its occurrence.

In order to maintain the body's production of heat and to prevent fatigue, special care should be taken to eat properly prior to the trip and while on the trail. A hot, hearty breakfast is especially important, and quick energy snacks such as candy, "gorp" or dried fruit should be munched while hiking. Hot meals should be eaten whenever possible.

Being physically fit does not, of itself, provide protection against hypothermia. However, a relatively high degree of fitness may delay the onset of fatigue and allow more heat producing work to be accomplished.

On the heat loss side of the balance, many precautions can be taken to prevent the excessive dissipation of body heat and subsequent hypothermia. The major protection against heat loss, of course, is to provide the body with adequate insulation.

Special care should be taken to provide coverage to the head and neck, since they will continue to lose heat by radiation even when vasoconstriction has reduced this loss elsewhere in the body. A light scarf or bandana around the neck will insulate the arteries and veins which lie close to the surface, and a hood or hat will protect the head. It has been shown that the head only requires about half the thickness of insulation required by the body to prevent a given amount of heat loss, so even a light cap can be helpful.

Still air is an excellent insulator. The effectiveness of down, synthetic fills, fishnet underwear and other insulations is primarily the result of their ability to trap and maintain a layer of dead air space around the body. Anything that will increase the thickness of this layer of dead air will improve the degree of insulation, and anything that reduces the thickness will destroy the insulation. A hiker who sits on a rock or even leans against a tree for long periods of time can become chilled even though he is completely encased in down-filled clothing. The pressure of his body will compress the down, thus reducing the insulating layer of air to almost nothing. At the same time, he will lose heat to the rock or tree by means of conduction. A similar situation exists beneath a sleeping bag which is placed directly on the ground or a thin tarp. In order to prevent the loss of heat as a result of compression of the insulation and conduction, additional "non-compressible" insulation must be placed beneath weight-bearing surfaces.

Convective heat loss can be a significant factor in the development of hypothermia, especially when wind is present. The insulation value of clothing is greatly reduced if the construction material is of loose weave and allows the wind to pass through. Ideally, loosely woven materials should be worn beneath windproof outer garments. The open materials will trap dead air for insulation, and the windproof material will prevent heat loss by convection.

Perhaps the most critical factor in the development of severe hypothermia is moisture. Wet clothing—whether from sweat, rain, or immersion—can rob the body of much needed heat in several ways. Most insulation loses a great deal of its value when it is wet. Down tends to mat and clump together and is all but worthless when it is soaked. Somewhat better in this respect are several of the newer synthetic insulation materials which retain their loft even when wet. The excess moisture can be squeezed from these materials and they will retain a portion of their insulating value even though damp. Wool has the rather unique property of drying from the inside out and is able to provide insulation and warmth when wet. Though it is heavy, it is a favorite of people who must work under damp conditions.

The major avenue of heat loss when wearing wet clothing is conduction. Since water conducts heat approximately 23 times faster than still air, the heat loss due to conduction through wet clothing that has already lost much of its insulating value is extremely large. Unfortunately, the most popular wearing apparel is also the most dangerous in this respect—cotton blue jeans. Jeans easily become soaked and virtually act as a wick to draw heat from the body. When wet clothing is also exposed to wind, the heat loss is compounded by both convection and evaporation, and hypothermia becomes almost a certainty.

It is absolutely imperative that the outdoorsperson make every effort to avoid becoming wet. Lightweight rain gear should be carried on *every* outing where there is even the most remote possibility of rain, lack of shelter and temperatures in the mid-50s or less. If stream crossings are necessary, the boots, socks and even the pants should be removed to keep them dry, and the body should be thoroughly dried before replacing them.

Wetness from perspiration is just as dangerous as moisture from rain or snow, and precautions should be taken to reduce the rate of sweating whenever possible. Several layers of light clothing should be worn rather than a single heavy layer. By opening or removing the clothing a layer at a time, the body temperature can be well controlled and sweating can be at least partially avoided. In additon, the layering of the clothing will trap air and provide extra insulation when needed. When attempting to reduce sweating, removal of the hat will help to dissipate unwanted heat by radiation. During cool to cold weather it is best to try to stay "just a hair warmer than chilly" while you are working, and then replace your hat and pile on the extra clothing to help retain body heat while you are resting.

Hypothermia is a very real threat to anyone who ventures into the outdoors, and all of us will at some time face the dangerous conditions which are conducive to massive heat loss: fatigue, rain, wind and temperatures in the mid-50s or below. The backpacker who is well-equipped and has a working knowledge of the body's heat producing and cooling mechanisms should have little cause to worry.

13 Rain Backpacking

Backpacking should be fair weather sport, but the elements don't always cooperate. The weather is especially unpredictable in the mountains. When you are hiking miles from civilized shelter, it is no time to discover that you cannot survive rain and cold.

Many years ago, as a novice hiker, I found out the hard way. Twenty miles from the road, we were hit by drenching rain and wind-whipped snow. In a warm shirt and a plastic raincoat I huddled with a friend under a flapping tarp. We had a choice to make: stay, get wet and freeze—or trudge to the car in one agonizing day.

We trudged; that night I slept in a wet sleeping bag after nursing blisters from soaked-through boots. I took the vow: never again would a storm catch me totally unprepared.

In those days, there were two additional options: get wet from the rain or get soaked by perspiration. A relatively new fabric (introduced commercially in 1976) solves that age-old dilemma. Gore-Tex, composed of a polytetrafluoroethylene (PTFE) membrane, is both breathable and waterproof. Many of today's leading manufacturers are using Gore-Tex

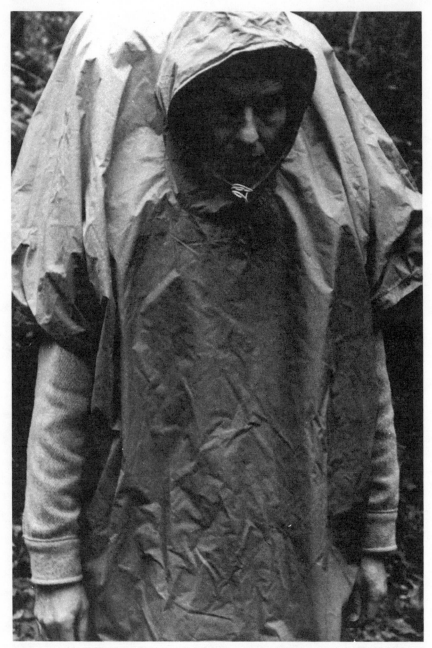

The popular packframe poncho covers all and ventilates, but for the coldblooded provides little wind protection.

in their rainsuits, parkas, tents, gloves and even boots. The one drawback, it seems, is the price; it's expensive. That's due to the use of three components in the Gore-Tex laminate. In addition, the PTFE membrane is a petrochemical derivative—subject to the price fluctuations of a limited number of suppliers.

Many people I know swear by the stuff; others are still skeptical. Speak to your local outfitter—and see what he recommends for your needs—before spending the extra bucks.

Another consideration when choosing rain gear is the disparity in each hiker's physical make-up. Some backpackers are like ambulatory furnaces. Others sport icicles when the temperature drops. To be effective, rain gear has to reflect these individual idiosyncrasies.

One soggy day in the mountains I met a burly guy whose answer to rain was to plop on a rain hat, then strip down to T-shirt and hiking shorts. His rain gear and dry clothes were tucked in his pack for use in camp only.

Most people, however, lack that polar bear mentality; but they do place high value on ventilation. Hooded ponchos provide maximum condensation relief. The walking-tent variety stretches to six feet in width. The most readily available size measures four and a half feet wide. It comes as either an under-the-pack model or as the pack frame design with extra-long back panel to cover hiker and pack. Judging from the grotesque, hunch-backed apparitions that roam trails on rainy days, I would say that the packframe poncho ranks number one in popularity.

Many hikers choose the narrow poncho. These are more compact, but they expose arms from the elbow down. One person I met had sewn a sleeve onto this type of poncho. Another friend made separate up-to-the-elbow sleeves with rubber at each end to be slipped on when needed.

There are additional problems to the poncho. During the last storm that I wore one, an icy wind whipped under my flowing cape. Even with a waist belt, I froze. I naturally concluded that adequate warmth was as important as ventilation. For "coldblooded" individuals, a jacket which can be wind-breaker and rainshield is the best choice.

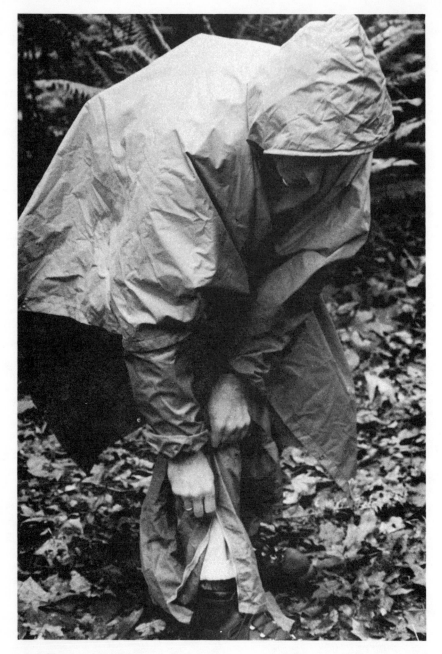

Waterproof materials can be purchased for making homemade rain gear or for adding to manufactured gear.

All jackets of coated-nylon steam up inside, so you must cope with this unwanted moisture. To absorb this condensation I wear a cotton shirt next to the jacket and put one or more layers of lightweight wool under that. Another hiker I know uses a cotton-lined rain jacket with layers of wool shirts, and he swears by the effectiveness of wool or cotton fishnet underwear next to the skin. Poncho users also survive cold rain with this "layered look."

Selection of clothing either worn or carried can obviously make a difference during storms. Old-fashioned jeans do not dry fast, but many dacron-cotton pants do. Synthetic shirts get clammy and cold. Cotton and wool are absorbent and remain more comfortable when damp. Wool provides more warmth even if wet.

There are jackets on the market which are 60-40 cotton and nylon, 50-50 cotton and nylon, or all cotton. These materials are water-repellent—not waterproof—and thus provide more ventilation. Recently I hiked with a friend who sported one of these mountain parkas. At camp we both waved our rain gear over the fire's heat. My waterproof variety was dry in minutes, while hers was still damp. She admitted that the jacket worked better in high altitude dry snow than in the rain.

Although I haven't decided about rain tops, I *have* decided that rain pants add a needed wind-proof layer. Just be sure a booted foot fits in easily before you buy. For the ventilation-minded, rain chaps are a good alternative. To minimize cost, either pants or chaps can be made at home with a simple pants pattern and a leg length of coated-nylon.

Another possibility for one piece rainwear is the cagoule, a jacket with an ankle-length skirt. The best principle for fitting jackets, pants or cagoules is to buy them large—more space and more air to combat that clammy feeling.

New rain gear is tricky. Wear it on day hikes, and don't be ashamed to test a new rain combination by standing under the backyard sprinkler. Your neighbors get a kick out of it, too.

On the trail, another important consideration is dry feet. Many hikers find that greasing boots with a warmed-on waterproofer stops leaks best. Boot design can be a factor. A friend bought a pair of very expensive boots only to discover that the tongue—which is a

Know yourself in choosing rain gear; if the windswept ventilation of a poncho isn't your thing, use a rain jacket but count on some condensation.

separate piece—leaks in heavy rain. In his old pair the tongue and the rest of the boot were constructed as one piece and folded under for closure to create a more watertight boot.

Although I always take a minimum of clean clothes, I don't scrimp on extra wool socks. Three or four pairs for a week are not too many. Then, if boots become damp inside, dry socks can restore comfort. In cold weather, I have also worn the extra socks as gloves.

That should suffice for the clothes you are *wearing*. But what about the gear you are carrying? Many packs are not that water-proof—especially in persistent rain. Old packs can become sieve-like with time and use. You can buy pack raincovers of plastic or coated nylon. They can also be made at home. Cut a circle of coated nylon large enough to cover the pack from shoulder strap to shoulder strap. Then hem it, thread thick rubber through the hem and pull the rubber tight enough to make it stay.

The best answer I have found to inside-the-pack dryness is to package everything in durable plastic bags. I had always put food in separate plastic coverings, and I usually had dry bread but wet clothes. With plastic bags for extra clothing and other loose gear, everything stayed dry with little weight added.

Sleeping bags are the most vital piece of equipment to keep dry. One miserable rainy morning last summer I met another party huddled around a fire at a sub-alpine camp.

"How's everything going?" I asked, just to be polite.

That casual remark unleashed a torrent of complaints, the biggest of which was that their down bags were soaked from the day before and even with a fire seemed undryable. Anyone who has washed down and spent many patient hours drying it can sympathize.

One of the most effective ways to protect a sleeping bag is to use a large, heavy-duty plastic bag—often sold as fish sacks. We put the fish bag on top of a coated-nylon stuffing sack and then squeeze in our ⅜-inch Ensolite pads. Plastic can tear but is easily repaired with electrical tape; these bags are inexpensive enough to replace.

On a stormy day, in-camp survival is as vital as on-the-trail comfort. For years I only slept under the stars and would carry only a light emergency tarp, which was the least expensive and most versatile type of protection. Several storms later, I realized that a tent is best for pitching camp fast and for withstanding severe wind and rain.

Like most hikers, I chose to buy rather than make. I found a tent which provides five by seven feet of floor space, enough room for two plus some gear. With ropes, stakes and fly it weighs only four and a half pounds. The tent itself is made of uncoated nylon that breathes. The floor and about eight inches up the sides are waterproof; the coated fly is constructed with no point of contact with the tent and uses separate stakes. The fly extends low to the ground in front of the zippered tent flap. With a low-pitched fly, getting in takes fancy wiggling—but neither can a storm creep inside too easily.

Slip a large heavy plastic bag into your pack to provide a second waterproof layer over sleeping bags if it rains.

A tent that pitches in minutes offers the best in-camp storm protection. A floorless tent ventilates; an enclosed tent requires a rain fly.

I have talked to several frugal backpackers who bought good tents, then successfully made a fly at substantial savings. One friend bought a tent fly which was too high and allowed front flap leakage. She added a diamond-shaped piece to the existing fly, and the tent became instantly watertight. An extended fly design also provides a vestibule in front of a crowded tent for cooking on a camp stove.

On a rainy day a campfire is beautiful, but it's a beautiful luxury. With an easy-to-light stove I can crawl into my tent for the duration.

Be sure to wrap a canister-type stove well inside your pack to insulate against cold, which will hamper its efficiency. Covering the canister in aluminum foil when using helps retain the workable temperature. On the windward side, extend the foil to the pot bottom to protect your flame.

You may ask why go to the trouble of being prepared for rain. Why not just pack out when the weather turns bad? Sometimes, of course, you are too far from the trail head. Generally, though, being rain-ready entails little preparation—and not too much additional weight. Knowing that you can comfortably survive a little unexpected rain is a good feeling before beginning the long trek to your destination.

When you arrive in camp on a rainy day, burrowing into a dry sleeping bag under adequate shelter is often the better part of valor.

14 *Direction Finding*

COMPASSES

A compass is a totally useless piece of equipment unless, of course, you know how to use one. If you understand the basics, then a compass could be of value in checking your position while on a hike. If you should become lost, a compass can help to show you the way back, providing that is, you know which direction you came from.

The chances of ever having to use a compass in an emergency situation are slim. But it is because of that one chance in a thousand that we all carry a compass. Knowing how to use a compass won't do you much good unless you know, either from experience or from looking at a map, where specific arteries—rivers, roads and trails—lead and are located, relative to your position. For this reason, a compass is most effective when used in conjunction with a topographical map.

There are three basic types of compasses that are popular with backpackers: floating-dial, fixed-dial and orienteering compasses.

The floating-dial compass is the easiest type of compass to use; you simply point the compass toward your destination (a landmark, for example), and read the indicated degree heading off the compass dial. This degree heading is read off the floating dial at an index mark inscribed into the base of the compass housing.

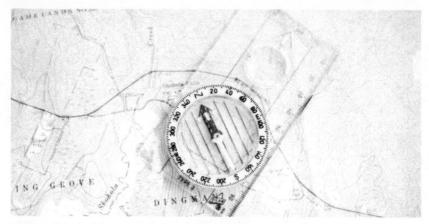

With map and compass orientated to magnetic north, point the compass at objective to find course (in this case the bearing is 62 degrees). *(Don Geary)*

Fixed-dial compasses are common "prizes" in Cracker Jacks and can only be depended on to find you the peanuts; their accuracy is rather dubious. Yet, because of the low price, many hikers carry this type of compass.

Orienteering compasses are the best bet for serious hikers. This type is easy to use—once you have spent about an hour familiarizing yourself with how it works. Basically, an orienteering compass is a floating needle type with degree markings inscribed on a rotating housing. This housing is mounted on a rectangular plate, usually made of clear plastic. Often one edge of the plate has inch markings while another edge will have millimeter markings. The clear plastic base and markings are an aid when working with a map.

Many compasses are filled with a liquid that dampens the movement of the dial or needle. Dampening will help the needle to come to rest more quickly and also prevents needle quiver. The liquid that is used for dampening will not freeze until the temperature drops below minus 40 degrees F.

The orienteering compass is still most useful when used in conjunction with a topographical map. The first step is to *orientate* the compass and map.

Along the bottom margin of all United States Geological Survey Maps there is a correction symbol for declination. Declination is the difference between true north and magnetic north, the latter being the direction your compass always points. The amount of declination can vary from 0 to almost 20 percent, east or west, depending on where you are located in North America. You will have to take declination into account if you want a true reading in relation to the map. If your objective is three miles off, for example, and you do not make a correction for declination (say 20 degrees), you will miss your mark by about a mile.

After the map and compass have been orientated to magnetic north, find your objective on the map. In most cases this will be a trailhead, road, river or lake. Next, point the arrow that runs down the center of your compass toward the objective. Then, while keeping the arrow pointing at your objective, turn the compass housing until the orienting arrow (part of the compass housing) lies directly below the compass needle. At this time, the compass needle will be pointing to magnetic north, the direction of travel arrow will be pointing at your objective (remember the map is orientated to magnetic north) and you can read the degree heading off the compass housing. This is the degree heading or bearing you will be following until you reach your objective.

When working with a map and compass, it is best to pick out a few landmarks that can be used to check your position and progress. For

The fixed-dial compass should be avoided, even though the price is right. *(Don Geary)*

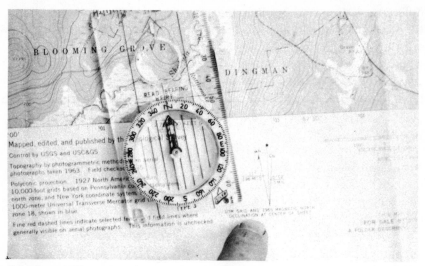

To orientate the map and compass, check the bottom of the map for declination correction. *(Don Geary)*

example, if you are heading for a lake, on a bearing of 200 degrees, look over the map to find obvious landmarks such as cliffs, streams, shelters or trails. As you hike across these points, you will have a good indication that you are pretty much on course.

Another good idea is to know, approximately, how far your objective is from your starting point. On all topographical maps there is a scale at the bottom of the map to tell you how many inches, for example, equal how many miles. Use the ruler on the side of your compass to measure the distance from starting point to objective and, with the use of the scale, convert the distance from inches to miles.

In open country, after you have determined your degree heading, look in that direction and try to find a landmark that lies approximately in the direction you want to go. As you walk, try to keep that landmark in view and head for it.

I mentioned earlier that a 20-degree error would amount to a miss of about a mile over a three-mile walk. Chances are good that there will be some error on all hikes for, in most cases, you cannot walk in a straight line. Trees, rocks and cliffs and things have a nasty way of popping up all the time in the wilderness. So you will probably be off a bit. But the idea is to be as close as possible. One degree of compass error amounts to about 90 feet over a distance of one mile. If you are heading for a small mountain pond of any size, you should be able to see it when you get in the general area.

In deep woods or forest, where it is not possible to use a landmark as a guide, you will have to check your compass frequently. This is most easily accomplished by holding the compass in the palm of your hand, as level as possible, and turning left or right until the needle of the compass points to magnetic north, and the bearing direction arrow points in the direction you want to travel. Even in thick terrain you should be able to pick out something in the general direction you want to travel. Walk for a while and then check the compass. Repeat this procedure as often as you feel necessary.

While you are using the compass, you should be aware that the needle that points to magnetic north will also be attracted by all kinds of iron and steel. This might include the contents of your pack, such as stove, belt buckle, pocket knife and even metal ore deposits around you. Incidentally, the filament in your flashlight bulb is an electromagnet that can deflect your compass needle. Keep this in mind if using your compass at night.

Always trust your compass to point to magnetic north. If you ever feel, for some reason, that you are not getting a true reading, there is a simple test that may help. Set the compass down on the ground, on top of a rock or stump, for example, and walk away. After a few minutes, slowly walk up to the compass. If the needle swings toward you, you probably have some steel or iron on your person.

Another rough check for a compass is possible when the sun is shining. You know that the sun rises in the east and travels in a westerly direction. Your compass needle should point in a perpendicular direction, relative to the sun's path.

If you have a wristwatch with a numbered dial, there is another check you can perform. No matter what time of day it is, if the sun is out, point the hour hand (the small one) at the sun. The direction of south lies halfway between the hour hand and the number 12.

Always carry a topographical map of the area you are hiking in, and check it often. Soon you will develop your map and compass reading ability to a point where you will feel confident.

Since most of the hiking that all of us do is on trails, either marked or well trodden, you probably won't ever have to use a compass except to satisfy your own curiosity. It is still a good idea to practice, however, just in case you ever have the desire to return to civilization.

TOPOGRAPHIC MAPS

Hiking backwoods trails with only the aid of conventional trail maps is comparable to motoring cross country only during the dark hours of the night. You get where you want to go, but you miss seeing much that would be of interest. Your observations as you walk along the nation's footpaths will take on new meaning if you supplement your trail guides with topographic maps prepared by the U.S. Geological Survey. But heed this warning: The study and use of topographic maps can be addictive; you may find yourself using them to plot a more interesting route to your neighborhood supermarket.

If you are not yet familiar with topographic maps, see if your local library has such maps of your area. However, be aware that many maps in library archives are old and not at all representative of the far more colorful and attractive modern versions. The new maps are so attractive that you may be tempted to do what a friend did many years ago—paper an entire wall with carefully matched quadrangles showing the area surrounding his home.

The primary value of any topographic map lies in the accurate and detailed information it provides about actual land contours. The countless brown, wavy lines that seem to wander aimlessly all over the map actually show where the land is relatively flat, where it rolls, and where there are hills or mountains. An experienced map reader can, furthermore, determine just how flat a given area is, how much it rolls and how steep a hill or mountainside is.

One way to visualize how contour lines can do all this is to imagine being on top of a mountain. Assume that you decide to use a *contour interval* of 40 feet, which means that each contour line you are about to draw will be 40 feet lower in elevation than the preceding one. (On some maps the contour interval is only ten feet; on others it may be 20 feet or some other convenient distance, depending on what scale the map maker chooses to use.)

From the highest point on the mountain move in any direction you wish until you are exactly 40 feet lower in elevation. Now draw a line on the surface of the mountain, at all times keeping it exactly 40 feet lower than the top. Your *horizontal* distance from the top will undoubtedly vary because the mountain is not symmetrical. Where the terrain slopes steeply, your contour line will travel quite close to the mountain top; where the slope is very gentle, the line will move much further away from the top. Eventually, you will arrive back at the starting point to complete a closed loop.

Having completed the first contour loop, draw another line 40 feet lower than the first. Then a third, another 40 feet lower, and so on until you have drawn rings all the way down the sides of the mountain and across the foothills. To see what you have done, rent a helicopter and hover over the mountain so that you can look straight down on the area as you would a map. You will note that all the loops are closed. In some places, they are bunched close together because there is a cliff face; in other places, they are much further apart because the land slopes gently.

How do you compute the height of the cliff? First note how many contour lines merge to form a thick single line where the cliff is located. Subtract one (to obtain the number of *intervals* between the lines), and multiply by the contour interval (40 feet) to calculate the height of the cliff. You can determine the vertical distance between any two points on the mapped area by multiplying the number of contour intervals between those points by the contour distance.

Symbols are the language of maps and are used to show where natural and man-made features are located. Unless the house in which you now live was built since the map for your area was last revised, you should find a small black square that marks the exact location of your home. If there is a small brook on your property, a blue line will show where it goes.

Approximately 100 different symbols are used to indicate the locations of such natural features as glaciers, sand dunes, rivers, swamps, springs, large river rapids, lakes, dry lake beds and woodlands; they are also used for such man-made features as roads, footpaths, canals, dams, buildings, mines, gravel pits, campsites, exposed shipwrecks, quarries and airports.

Of what value is all this information? It depends on what is of interest to you. If you are a rock and mineral collector, you may be interested in making side trips to potential collecting locations such as old mines, quarries, gravel pits, streams, or even exposed cliff faces. A fisherman will want to know where to find that off-the-trail pond or stream that has not yet been discovered by hordes of other anglers. Or maybe you enjoy canoeing. A topographic map will help you find the most direct routes across lakes; it will aid in the search of good campsites and will indicate the locations of small streams to explore when the main routes no longer offer new challenges. Note, however, that topographic maps usually show only major rapids in the larger rivers; an uninterrupted blue line does not necessarily mean that a given stream will provide smooth, mill-pond canoeing conditions. Other maps may indicate where portage routes are located; your topographic map will reveal how rough or smooth these portages will be.

Every now and then you will run into features that you find particularly interesting but that are not marked on the map. If you mark the exact location on your map, you will be able to find the same spot years later—even when accurate memory of the precise location has faded away.

If you stick to the beaten path, a topographic map can still have good uses. For example, the question may arise whether you should stop at the campsite you have just reached or push on to the next one. Your topographic map will reveal how much climbing will be involved and whether the terrain around the second campsite might offer better shelter from an approaching storm.

Each topographic map represents a quadrangle bounded by parallels of latitude and meridians of longitude. Quadrangles covering 7½ minutes of latitude and longitude are published at the scale of 1:24,000. This means that one inch on the map is equivalent to 2,000 feet. Quadrangles covering 15 minutes of latitude and longitude are at the scale of 1:62,500; here, one inch is equivalent to about one mile. Other scales are used on a few special maps.

The 1:24,000 scale is used for areas, such as urban centers, where considerable detail must be shown; mountain country and other relatively unpopulated areas are likely to be in the 1:62,500 scale. In some instances you can obtain maps in either scale, so it's important that you clearly specify which you want. The free index map that shows how your state is broken down into individual map areas may reveal such scale options. If you were simply to ask for the Skaneateles quadrangle in New York State, you might receive a 15-minute map that shows a larger area than you care about, or a 7½-minute map that represents only one-fourth of the actual land area covered by the 15-minute map. Only a large scale map, covering a smaller area, might contain the detailed information you need.

The topographic map is useful for developing what I call "sweat profiles." These will give you some advance knowledge about the difficulty of particular parts of the trail. The profile of the Long Trail illustrates the kind of information you can quickly obtain from a topographic map.

The "crow-flight" distance from the starting point to the peak is about 5,000 feet. For the first 3,500 feet or so the trail stays pretty much between the 3,200 and 3,240 foot contour lines, so you know that the going will be very easy. The trail then begins to climb, and you can deduce that there is a fairly constant slope from the 3,400 to the 3,800 foot elevation because the contour lines are fairly evenly spaced. Near the top the contour lines are packed closer together because the trail climbs more steeply.

From the 3,200 foot elevation to the 4,083 foot peak you face an increase of 683 feet in elevation over a horizontal (not actual trail) distance of about 1,200 feet. If you remember your elementary trigonometry, you know that dividing 683 by 1200, gives you the tangent of the angle formed by the trail and the horizontal base line—(0.569). Looking up 0.569 in your trig tables, you will find that the average gradient of this part of the trail is a little less than 30 degrees. There's even a simpler method to arrive at the same answer. Just draw a right angle on a sheet of paper, and mark off 1,200 units on the base line and 683 on the vertical leg. Complete the triangle, and measure the angle with a protractor. Want a still simpler estimate? Divide both numbers by 100. Your answers (12 and 6.8) tell you that for every 12 feet you move ahead (in terms of the horizontal base line) you must go upward close to seven feet.

Incidentally, if you should want to draw similar profiles and relate them to tracings of contour lines made from your map, be sure to use the same graphic units to represent both horizontal and vertical distances. Otherwise, your profile will be unrealistic. Note also that the example shown here does not represent a cross section of the mountain; the purpose was to develop a profile of the *trail* itself.

Relate maps to experience on the trails. This is necessary if you want to obtain the greatest benefit and fun from them. Keep a log of actual travel times along various sections of the trail. In time you will be able to anticipate with much greater certainty how much faster you travel along level ground than uphill.

This kind of information is of particular importance to people who engage in competitive outdoor activities, such as orienteering. This sport involves walk/run foot races over pre-planned courses. Since competitors must find various check points with the aid of map and compass, knowing which of two alternate routes is quicker could make a big difference.

Although some map stores and larger camping supply outlets—in particular those specializing in mountaineering supplies—stock limited selections of topographic maps, the odds are that you will have to do much of your shopping by mail order. Maps of areas east of the Mississippi River—including Minnesota, Puerto Rico and the Virgin Islands—should be ordered from the Branch of Distribution, U.S. Geological Survey, 1200 South Eads Street, Arlington, VA 22202. Maps of areas west of the Mississippi River—including Alaska, Hawaii, Louisiana, American Samoa and Guam—should be ordered from the Branch of Distribution, U.S. Geological Survey, Federal Center, Denver, CO 80225.

These distribution centers will provide state map indices free of charge. Each index shows the entire state and the sections into which it has been divided. The index also provides a list of retail outlets which supply maps of the state and a list of libraries that have topographic maps (this way you can photocopy map sections of interest). Most topographic maps now cost about $1 each when ordered from the government distribution centers; the same maps will cost anywhere from $1.50 to $3.25 or more through retail outlets. Be sure to ask for a free descriptive booklet that describes the symbols used on topographic maps. In years past these symbols were printed on the back sides of all maps, but not so today.

15 Cooking

FOOD AND UTENSILS

Moths may never fly out of your dehydrated carrots, and still your backpacking trip may turn into a digestive disaster unless you understand some basic facts about living off the land.

I assume you have no intention of turning your backpacking trip into a grim survival experiment wherein you subsist on wild onions, lizard steaks and coconuts. All you plan to do is take a pleasant, extended walk through the woods, maybe climb a mountain or two, and eat civilized meals that you carry on your back. But still, in a very real sense you *will* be living off the land because there's one vital consumable that must be obtained from the land through which you travel. It's *water.*

As for that seeming nonsense about moths in carrots, let me assure you that it is possible. Or at least *was* possible back in the days when Horace Kephart, rather than Colin Fletcher, was the great guru of outdoor lore. There was no dashing out to the local supermarket or even to a camping supply store to pick up factory-dehydrated foods. You made your own by drying thinly-sliced vegetables in your kitchen oven. The results varied from "passable" to "yuk," but it was all gulped down with pretended relish.

The point I have been leading up to is this. Back in the days when you might have found moths in your carrots, it was possible to drink deeply from mountain brooks without much fear of becoming ill. Today, when you can buy an endless variety of nutritious, palatable and guaranteed vacuum and freeze-dried foods from your local supermarket, you must be *very* cautious about putting lip to burbling brook. Even when you know there are no permanent human habitations upstream, you are not necessarily safe. Why? Because up there on the ridge trail there is now likely to be an almost constant flow of foot travelers, many of whom seem to think that mountain brooks were divinely created for the sole purpose of carrying away all forms of man-made wastes. You don't have to go south of the border to suffer Montezuma's Revenge or its equivalent. It's bad enough to deal with a roiled-up digestive system when at home, but far worse when you are on a wilderness mountain trail.

Be sure that you know how to purify *all* the water you consume, whether directly or through cooking your food. Boiling your water is one way to ensure that all harmful bacteria, viruses and parasites are killed. Just remember to boil water longer than the usual ten minutes when you are at high elevations where the boiling temperature of water is significantly lower. Often it is just too inconvenient to purify water by boiling. For example, when you want to refill your canteen from a brook during the middle of the day. In this case drop a Halazone tablet into the canteen and the water, if it is not abnormally polluted, will be fit for drink in a half hour. Each small Halazone tablet will sanitize one pint of water.

At times you will find that available water supplies are contaminated with various kinds of suspended materials such as silt, clay, aquatic life forms such as algae and non-vegetable microorganisms, partly-decayed vegetation and other less easily identifiable crud. Filtration is the only answer, but you may find that much of the finer suspended matter will pass through a cloth or paper towel filter. You can still use the coffee-colored water after boiling, but it isn't very appetizing. To avoid this unpleasant situation, provided you are willing to pay up to about 50 cents per gallon for pure water, invest in a water purification device. Retail prices currently range from about ten dollars and up for a pack (about the size of a raisin box when rolled up for carrying) which will purify up to 20 gallons of water, maybe even as much as 30 gallons if the water is fairly clean initially. Advertising blurbs for such equipment state that by passing water through the large-diameter tube made of flexible plastic and the enclosed purifier system, you can remove such contaminants as dirt, bacteria, slime, microorganisms, scale, virus, parasites, detergents, rust, algae and various mineral and chemical components. It's said to deliver up to half a pint of water per minute, but is *not* suitable for purifying salt water. Although it's claimed that the device is effective in killing 99.5 percent of common water-born bacteria including Escherichia coli and various forms of Salmonella, I'd still be inclined to drop a Halazone tablet into heavily polluted water, after filtration, especially if the purifying device has already seen much use.

The food you carry into the wilderness should be nutritious, tasty, easy to prepare, as light in weight as possible and packaged so as to simplify waste-disposal problems. If you are a novice backpacker, your main problem will be deciding how much of what to take so that you won't go hungry, won't waste energy carrying too much food and won't fall dead on some remote wilderness trail because of a marginal vitamin deficiency.

There are those who just aren't happy unless they work out an entire trip menu on a strictly "scientific" basis, taking into account calorie counts and the nutritional values of various foods. These are the people who feel frustrated if they still have three raisins left over when they complete the trip. I am not knocking this approach, because I think there is nothing inherently wrong about it. But I do think that it's largely a waste of time unless you are planning to climb Mt. Everest or intend to jog the full length of the 2,000-mile Appalachian Trail.

I would suggest that you adopt a common sense approach. Shop for good *dehydrated* foods at your local supermarket, camping supply dealer and in the pages of leading mail-order suppliers of camping needs. Work toward a reasonable balance of carbohydrates (sugars and starches), fats, and proteins—let's say in about 3-1-1 ratio. Test unfamiliar foods in your home, before the trip, so you will know how easy they are to prepare, how good they taste and how filling a typical "serving" really is (don't rely on what the manufacturer says about the number of servings). Remember that vigorous outdoor exercise will make you much hungrier than you are normally, so plan generous portions for all persons in your party.

The kinds of foods to look for include dried soups, meat bars, dried fruits, dehydrated potatoes and other vegetables, powdered non-fat milk, raisins, hard candy, chocolate candy (preferably the tropical variety that won't melt into a gooey mess in your pack or pocket), fruit drink mixes, margarine, sugar, tea and/or coffee, salt and pepper, dry cereals (avoid space-wasting cereals like corn flakes which are mostly air, and go for the Swiss-type cereals that include fruits and nuts).

Also see what special concentrated foods you can find at your local camping supply store or in supplier catalogs. They are likely to be high priced, but their nutritional values in relation to carrying weights may make them attractive nonetheless. For example, high-energy fruit pemmican consisting of a mixture of seedless raisins, peanuts, apples and dextrose (a quickly assimilable sugar) is a tasty quick-energy food that is ideal for an on-the-trail snack. A can holding about three and a quarter ounces costs about $1. A meat pemmican bar weighing three ounces, and selling for $3.50, is claimed to provide over 500 calories and is said to be the equivalent of a half pound of raw meat. Other specialty items include beef jerky, a smoke-dried beef you can chew on the trail or use to spike a stew; apricots, prunes and other fruits in handy sheet form; even Army K-ration chocolate nut rolls for dessert. If some prices seem too steep, you may find ways to obtain approximate equivalents at lower cost. For example, ordinary fruit cake would be a good substitute for fruit pemmican.

Bear in mind that eating nothing but concentrated foods can throw your digestive system out of kilter and lead to either constipation or diarrhea. To avoid these problems, work in foods that provide some roughage—cereals or green fresh vegetables that will keep for a few days without refrigeration. Also plan your menu with the kind of country through which you will be traveling in mind. If the trail frequently crosses main highways and passes near or through villages, you can count on picking up fresh fruits, vegetables and meats along the way. On the other hand, if your trail keeps entirely to wilderness areas, you must pack in your entire food supply from the start.

Do *not* count on supplementing your diet with wild foods you hope to find in the woods unless you are knowledgeable in this practice. If you find foods you are sure you recognize (wild strawberries or blueberries, for example) they can be pleasant additions to your diet. But if you are in doubt about the edible qualities of any plant, leave it alone.

Many ordinary foods need repackaging at home to reduce bulk and/or weight. Seal bulk foods like cereals in double-weight plastic freezer bags and look for lightweight plastic containers for smaller volume items. Your camping supply shop may have those handy plastic squeeze tubes that *you* can fill with pasty foods such as peanut butter, jam and honey. Not only are they light in weight and handy to use, but they keep foods clean even if dropped.

Avoid using metal and glass containers as much as possible. If you are any kind of civilized wilderness traveler, you need not be told how important it is that you *bring back with you everything that you cannot either eat or burn.*

If you will be on the trail any length of time, consider also a plastic roll-up type of water bag. Some models hold over two gallons of water and have handy drain spigots.

Do not plan on supplementing your diet with wild foods unless you are knowledgeable in this practice. These little puffballs are only *slightly* poisonous. *(Judith N. Moyer)*

If you intend to do your cooking on an open fire, be sure that you know how to build fires, contain them safely and control them for cooking. (See following sections for fire-building *and* backpacking stoves.)

Carry only as many pots and other cooking utensils as you actually need to prepare the foods you will carry. Don't forget to include a length of clothesline or other light but strong rope in your cooking gear, if you do not already have it on your list for other reasons. Use the rope to suspend your foodstuffs between a couple of trees during the night, so that wild animals can't get at your precious supplies—especially when you are in bear country. Moths in your carrots would be good for a laugh, but a bear in your larder would be a disaster.

FIRE-BUILDING

Exactly how primitive men started their fires we don't know; they *probably* rubbed two pieces of the right kind of wood together—two pieces that were bone dry. (This "right kind of wood" is too rare for contemporary fire-builders.) Or, perhaps, the old-timers used the "flint and steel" trick, which required a hard stone such as flint, obsidian, agate or quartzite as well as charred cloth with which the spark would ignite.

For our purposes, if we intend to resort to fire by friction, it is advisable that one of the sticks be a match.

The modern-day kindler must also be aware of his or her ecological surroundings; a campfire is indeed magical, but is it *necessary?* If you do choose to build one, do it with minimal impact on the environment.

The first thing to remember is that you don't need rocks to make an efficient and safe fire. You can make a serviceable fireplace—that will disappear after you've gone—by digging one in the ground.

Start by removing the sod and topsoil from a 12-by-16-inch rectangle of ground. Set aside in a pile. Next, dig down about six inches until you reach mineral soil, which contains nothing that can catch fire. In this fire pit you can build your fire.

If available, three types of wood are now needed: tinder, kindling and fuel wood. Tinder is used to begin the fire: dry grass, rotten bark, dry pine cones, pitch and small twigs. If it has recently rained,

Begin the fire structure by making a "H" of one-half inch sticks. *(Betty Hughes)*

With mouth at fire level, blowing up through the fire (rather than down onto it) will speed its growth. *(Betty Hughes)*

find a dead birchbark tree; peel some of the bark away. The second and third layers should be dry. Birchbark, once used by American Indians for canoes, is waterproof; it insures that the inside bark structure and wood will stay dry. Also, the bark flares up—like small sparklers or a pinch of gunpowder.

The fire structure should be a small "H" pattern—two parallel pieces of half-inch sticks with a "crossbar" lying across the two. Lay more tinder against the crossbar on both sides, forming an "A" shape. Stack it well, but leave air circulation space for oxygen. The need for oxygen is greater when the wood is wet.

If the wood is too wet, the structure should be built over a piece of candle, which should burn for about ten minutes. Above the tinder, add only a dozen pieces of the smallest kindling. You will have to nurse the tinder and kindling once it ignites; again, the length of time is determined by how wet the wood is. Do not add too much kindling, or fuel wood too soon, or you will smother the flame.

Before you light your little structure, a word about matches. When provisioning for your trip, plan for the contingency of wet weather. This means waterproofing your wooden kitchen matches by either coating them with melted paraffin or painting them with clear fingernail polish. Paraffin is preferable because it burns with a hot blaze. Nail polish tends to spit and sputter. Take care to submerge the entire length of the match in the hot paraffin; any exposed wood will absorb water by capillary action, leaving the match useless.

For each fire you plan to make, take ten matches—half in your pocket and the rest in your pack. You might also make your own candles by tightly rolling newspaper into candle thickness, binding it with light wire, sawing it into one-inch lengths and thoroughly saturating with paraffin. A piece of twine inside the roll acts as a wick.

Once your structure is ready for lighting, hold the match well under tinder—or light the candle if needed—being careful not to knock the little thing down. Holding an evergreen twig along with the match will prolong its burning time. Once the flame catches, keep adding kindling; blowing gently on it can increase the heat of the flame and help it grow. Add larger kindling; then begin adding the smaller fuel wood until the fire is going on its own steam.

There's a philosophy to tending fires which distinguishes the tenderfoot from the woodsperson. The Indians summed it up: "The white man builds a big fire, wastes wood and sits far away from the flame. The Indian builds a small fire, saves wood and sits close to the flame."

16 Backpacking Stoves

To be sure, nothing quite equals the warmth and comfort of a roaring fire after a day in the outdoors; then again, nothing quite equals the efficiency and dependability of a good hiking stove.

There are several reasons why you should carry a small backpacking stove every time you go on an overnight hike. Probably the most obvious is that you know that you will always be able to boil water for meals and, in a pinch, you can use the stove to quickly warm up your tent.

By using a stove you have a lot more freedom; that's what backpacking is about. You are not limited to areas where there is an abundance of firewood. You can also cover more territory, knowing that you don't have to stop an hour early to set up camp and perform all the related tasks—building a suitable place for a campfire, cutting and collecting firewood and then tending a fire.

There is also the obvious environmental concern. With so many people on the trails, it is becoming increasingly important that each of us uses less of the wilderness areas. That means specifically firewood. I have hiked into remote areas of the Adirondack

Mountains and been quite surprised at the lack of available firewood. Usually, in wilderness areas, the forest floor is cluttered with dead trees and branches which are ideal for a campfire. Greater use of state and federal trails results in, among other things, less firewood in certain areas. Campfires also leave a black scar on the wilderness floor.

So, in the name of environmental causes, efficiency and dependability, I always carry a small backpacking stove.

Just one look at any of the equipment catalogs or in any specialty shop should be enough to confuse you about hiking stoves. Prices range from 25 to 90 dollars, and many of the stoves seem to be about the same. In an effort to learn more about backpackers' stoves, you should know that there are two basic types: liquid fuel and bottled fuel.

Liquid fuel stoves are traditionally the most dependable, most expensive and most popular type of hiking stove. There are three kinds of liquid fuel burning stoves: alcohol, kerosene and white gas burners.

Alcohol (denatured) burns much cooler than the other two types of liquid fuel. It is also the most expensive, costing about four dollars a gallon. The attraction of alcohol lies in the fact that it is safer to use than the other two types, and it is readily available all over the world. Flame burning alcohol will produce about half as much heat as a flame burning white gas or kerosene; this means that you'll have to carry twice as much alcohol to get the same heat output.

Kerosene burns hotter than the other two types of liquid fuel; it is less volatile and is inexpensive, costing less than a dollar per gallon. However, kerosene tends to give off a bit of foul smelling smoke while it burns and, because it is less volatile than alcohol or white gas, it can be difficult to ignite at times.

White gas is, by far, the most popular type of liquid fuel for backpacking stoves. White gas is actually an additive-free version of regular automobile gasoline. The real thing is nearly impossible to find in most parts of the country, so most hikers use Coleman Fuel. Coleman Fuel is really better than white gas because the folks at Coleman make it specifically for campstoves. It contains additives and rust inhibitors that make for easy lighting and just about eliminates fouling of internal working parts. Current cost is under two dollars per gallon. Coleman fuel is available in gallon size containers at every hardware store in the country. I have never had a problem finding it anywhere in the United States or Canada.

White gas (and Coleman Fuel) is potentially dangerous, and you should always be cautious when using a stove that burns this type of fuel. Be especially wary when you are refueling the stove and when first lighting the burner.

The other general type of hiking stove is one that burns bottled fuel—either propane or butane. These fuels come in pressurized steel containers. The obvious advantage of using a stove that burns this type of fuel is convenience. The fuel canister is either pushed or screwed into the stove, and the burner is ready to light.

It would seem that containerized fuel stoves would be safer than liquid burning stoves. Not quite. Although the manufacturers take pains to insure that these stoves will work well at all times, the possibility always remains for a poor connection between the burner and the fuel canister. Since you cannot *see* the fuel, you could be in for a real surprise if the connection is poor and leaking fuel when you light the stove.

I have been detailing propane and butane as if they were the same type of fuel; they are not. The main difference between the two is the temperature at which they will vaporize. Butane is actually better suited for warmer weather; at temperatures below 32 degrees Fahrenheit it will not vaporize. Propane, on the other hand, will keep on working down to minus 44 degrees.

As the fuel in a container of butane vaporizes and burns, the canister will cool and the stove's efficiency is reduced. Continuously burning a butane fired stove will take a real bite out of the efficiency of that stove—to the point of decreasing, by half, the heat output. However, for normal meal preparation, where the stove is used for short periods and then shut off, the efficiency will be barely affected.

Propane is less affected by cold weather because of the greater internal pressure of the fuel. Unfortunately, this pressure means that the propane can only be put into a container that is strong and in most cases, heavy. Propane's real value becomes apparent at high, cold altitudes and not for three-season casual hiking.

WHITE GAS STOVES

I have been using a small, white gas burner for several years. My Svea is compact (five by 3¾ inches in diameter) and weighs around 22 ounces with a full tank of fuel. The Svea will boil a quart of water inside of ten minutes, depending, of course, on freshness of fuel, altitude and weather conditions. With a full tank of fuel, the Svea will burn for about an hour, more than enough time to cook just about any type of trail meal you can think of.

I have been using the stove for such a long while that I tend to overlook the disadvantages. For one thing, the Svea cooks hot. This is great for boiling water, the main ingredient for reconstituting freeze-dried meals. Cooking other types of foods requires a special knack, however, or part of the meal will end up as a black mess on the bottom of the cook pot.

The Svea (and other types as well) can be difficult to start when it is very cold; it is advisable to insulate the stove from snow or cold. I have found that the best method of insulation is to set the stove on a corner of an Ensolite pad. If a cold wind is blowing, I use the stove in a tent or rig up some type of protection—laying my pack between the stove and winds, for example.

Every white gas burning hiking stove will occasionally start to sputter. This usually means that there is some type of gum buildup in the burner orifice, and it must be cleaned out. I clean out the Svea with a tool that was supplied with the stove. It looks like a miniature folding pocket knife but has a pin instead of a blade. Simply unfold the tool, push the pin into the orifice hole, and move it up and down to dislodge any buildup of gum. The new Svea and several other stoves (Optimus 8R, for example) have a pin inside the stove. To clean out the orifice, the control knob is simply turned further as the pin comes up from the inside.

All white gas burning stoves operate about the same. With the Svea, the fuel tank is filled first. This requires either a very steady hand or a fuel bottle with a special pouring spout. Needless to say, you should not fill the stove around any open flame. It also makes sense to fill the stove away from the area where you plan to do your cooking. If you should spill some of the fuel on the stove body, wait about five minutes before trying to light the stove. White gas evaporates rapidly when exposed to fresh air.

Once the stove has been filled and the fuel tank cap securely fastened, you can begin preheating the stove. With the exception of the new Coleman Peak One stove, most white gas burners do not have a pump to pressurize the fuel tank. Therefore, the fuel in the tank must be heated slightly; this causes the fuel to expand and be forced through a tiny aperture, where it is then burned. Once the stove is burning properly, the heat from the flame will generally be enough to keep the stove running efficiently.

There are several methods of preheating a white gas burning stove. I have found it easiest to simply pour a few drops of fuel into the burner cup and touch a match to the stove. The flame will cause the stove parts to heat up enough to expand the fuel in the stove tank. Just about the time the flame goes out, I turn the stove on.

There are a few simple safety rules to follow when preheating a stove in this fashion. First, don't preheat the stove in a tent. When the stove is running properly, it can then be brought into the tent. Second, don't put more than five or six drops of fuel into the burner cup. Some hikers like to use an eyedropper for putting the few drops of fuel onto the burner.

A special cleaning tool is supplied with older model Sveas. *(Don Geary)*

Filling should always be done with a funnel or special pouring spout cap. *(Don Geary)*

161

Once the stove has been preheated and is burning as it should, you can use it for boiling water or cooking. Most white gas burners are efficient little blowtorches with not very much of a simmer control. The exception, as mentioned earlier, is the new Coleman Peak One.

The Peak One stove is a bit heavy, weighing around 34 ounces with a full tank (ten ounces of fuel). The Peak One is also slightly bigger than the Svea, being 6½ inches high and 4⅝ inches in diameter. The excess weight and slightly larger size are offset by the performance of the stove. The Peak One will boil a quart of water in under six minutes. It will burn for about an hour and ten minutes at full blast. The unique simmer control enables you to run the stove on low flame for over 3½ hours.

Another appealing feature of the Peak One is that the stove does not need preheating the way other white gas burners do. The fuel tank is pressurized by a Coleman pressure pump system.

BUTANE STOVES

The Primus Ranger is one of the most efficient heat producers of the butane stoves. It is a collapsible tripod affair, with two legs under the burner and the third leg consisting of the fuel canister and burner adjustment. It will burn for approximately four hours on a can of butane, bringing a quart of water to boil in under ten minutes. With a full cannister of butane, the Primus Ranger weighs about 18 ounces. It folds down for carrying to 3 inches diameter by 12.5 inches long. It is very easy to light under normal mild weather conditions and has an easy to use burner control.

Like every other type of stove, the Primus Ranger has a few weak points. It has no windscreen, so it doesn't work well in an open area. It also has a high center of gravity, but the long legs do a nice job of holding things up. Butane burners are not a very good choice in cold weather, being susceptible to flareups when lighting and marked loss of efficiency when burned for extended periods. Nevertheless, the Primus Ranger is a very worthwhile backpacking stove for those that want the convenience of containerized fuel.

The Primus stove is simple to operate. First, a container of butane is carefully screwed into the control mechanism, and the stove is ready for use. The proper way to light the Primus (and any other

Stove	Price	Fuel	Weight	Weight with fuel	Height (inches)	Width (inches)	Length (inches)	Fuel Cap. (ounces)	Boiling Time (minutes)
Bluet S-200	$27	Butane	1 lb.	1 lb., 11 ozs.	4½	3½	9½	6.3	5
MSR Multi-Fuel	$80	Almost anything	1 lb.	2 lb.	3½	3¼	9	16/32	4
Optimus 8R	$48	White gas	1 lb., 7 ozs.	1 lb., 10 ozs.	3¼	5	5	3.2	7
Optimus 111B	$90	White gas	3 lbs., 8 ozs.	4 lbs., 14 ozs.	4	6¾	7	16	6
Coleman Peak 1	$40	White gas	1 lb., 15 ozs.	2 lbs., 9 ozs.	6½	4⅝	—	10	6
Hank Roberts Mini	$30	LP gas	8 ozs.	1 lb., 1 oz.	—	4½	1½	6.2	6
Svea 123R	$44	White gas	1 lb., 2 oz.	1 lb., 6 oz.	5	4½	—	6	6

(Courtesy of Thunderbird Tepee outfitters, Brooklyn, NY)

stove) is to strike a match and hold the flame next to the burner; then turn the gas on. Never turn the gas on and *then* light the match; this could result in a flareup or worse.

Your choice of a hiking stove should be based on how much hiking you actually do, when you hike, the type of food you normally bring along (if only freeze-dried, your only requirement will be fast, boiling water) and how much you are willing to spend. Most butane stoves cost around $25-30 and are geared for three-season hikers. They do tend to be less efficient than white gas burners and certainly more expensive to run.

White gas stoves range in price from 40 dollars upward. They are efficient at most temperatures and usually dependable.

If you hike only in mild weather and don't mind paying a bit more for fuel, then a butane stove is probably for you. On the other hand, if you do a lot of hiking all year round and need a dependable stove, you won't mind paying a little more for a quality white gas burner.

Whichever type of stove you choose, there are several rules that should always be followed for safe operation. Use your stove at home a few weeks before you plan to hike. This way if the stove does not work properly you can have it repaired by a qualified repair shop.

When you are on the trail or in camp, always make sure that the stove sits on a level surface. The area around the stove should be cleared of all combustible materials, such as pine needles and leaves. Of course, spare fuel should be kept out of the direct rays of the sun and well away from the burning stove. Try to position the stove in a place where it is least likely to get bumped over.

If you must use the stove inside your tent, make sure there is adequate ventilation. Carbon monoxide is a by-product of all stoves; adequate ventilation is not only a good idea, it is a necessity. Most tents have some type of venting system; make sure it is working. You should leave the tent door open, at least partially, for cross ventilation. If your tent does not have some type of venting, don't use the stove inside the tent.

Use the correct fuel for your stove. If it is a white gas burner, stick with Coleman fuel. Never use automobile gasoline; this fuel may work for a while, but it will kill your stove in a short time. If your stove uses butane or propane, use the type of canister recommended by the manufacturer. Some of the accidents that occur are, in most cases, the result of the wrong fuel canister being used.

With butane or propane stoves, the fuel canister should never get hot; in fact the fuel supply container should always seem cool to the touch. Touch the container often when using the stove. If it is ever hot to the touch, turn the stove off.

Never prevent free air circulation around any stove; this might cause excessive heat buildup. Never, for example, surround a stove with rocks to protect it from the wind.

Never refill a hot stove. Let it cool first. When replacing fuel canisters, be careful. Most fittings are made from brass and can be stripped without too much effort. If the canister is installed incorrectly, it will leak. One way to check for leaks is, again, to touch the canister. If it feels frosty, you have a leak and should check your connection.

A small stove, either white gas or butane fired, is a necessary piece of equipment for serious hiking. A little bit of caution while you are operating the stove will insure that the stove does its job efficiently and safely.

17 Trail Hygiene

Many people who hear the *Call of the Wild* never try backpacking along wilderness trails because they worry excessively about coping with the *Call of Nature.* Outdoor writers who largely ignore or gloss over supposedly "delicate" sanitation and hygiene problems may justify their silences with the knowledge that even the rankest novice will quickly find a solution when the needs arise. But that's no help for those who need answers and reassurances *before* they venture into the woods.

Every aspiring woodsperson should know of these problems and the civilized solutions to them, for two reasons. Backpacking is more fun for those who go properly prepared mentally and physically; secondly, more publicity about the importance of wilderness sanitation is needed to keep the despoilers of nature at a minimum.

With these objectives in mind, let's begin with a question: What kinds of rest rooms can be found in the wilderness?

Backwoods sanitary facilities can be classified into four general types: primitive, more primitive, intolerable and non-existent. A reasonably clean pit toilet or "privy" can be considered a luxury even though it may be so primitive as to lack a door. If the assumed

165

lack of privacy is disturbing, be assured that a soft whistling or humming will provide all the privacy you crave.

Also, a doorless privy is likely to be cleaner, because it receives better airing, provided it is located where there are few or no animal pests. For example, porcupines will chew anything that tastes even slightly salty, and that includes toilet seats. At times there are other aesthetic reasons why you will happily do without a door. I don't know if it's still there, but years ago one could sit at the very top of the highest mountain in the Adirondacks and reflect on the majestic scenery around Mt. Tahawus (Indian meaning "Cloud Splitter"). If you can't find Tahawus on the map it's because this imaginative name was long ago changed to Mt. Marcy.

A more primitive type of facility might be a simple seat somewhere in the bushes, with *no* concealing walls. When using these, you whistle or hum just a bit louder. The advantage of the open-plan toilet is that it is the most efficiently air-conditioned facility you will find ready for use. The most luxurious open-plan privy I have ever encountered was the *porcelain* fixture that someone had backpacked all the way to the top of a Vermont mountain. The porcupines had left only the hinges of the original wooden seat.

An "intolerable" facility is one that is unusable because of misuse by people who can only be charitably characterized as *slobs*, or because some form of wildlife has appropriated the privy. Look over the door on the inside before entering; you might find a bees' nest.

For the benefit of the more adventurous readers still with us, I'll hasten to add that when you find unacceptable facilities or none at all, you can get along very well with your own do-it-yourself rest room—provided you know how to go about making one. One further warning, though. Carry your own paper; there are no regular attendants for even the best of backwoods' rest rooms. Roll paper is most convenient for laying on the privy seat to ensure added sanitation, but a roll is awkward to carry in a pocket unless it is mostly used up and squashed as flat as possible. Packets of individual sheets pack better, but you must remember to remove the sheets only as you need them.

Now for a few tips about do-it-yourself wilderness rest rooms. We don't deliberately want to offend any delicate sensibilities, but there is no quaintly euphemistic and simultaneously clear way to say what needs saying. If you plan a diet that keeps your digestive track functioning efficiently, you can usually cope with the call of nature just by squatting. If you need more time, or your knee joints tire easily, you need something on which to sit. *That,* incidentally, is what bugs fastidious non-camping women especially; they can't imagine where one would sit in the woods.

If you are in a forest, you can often find a downed tree or branch that can be used as a seat, or you can lash a sturdy section of tree limb between a couple of small trees. If the bark is loose, peel it off before using to make sure that there are no insects lurking underneath. Also, avoid branches of evergreen trees because the resinous pitch is hard to get off skin or clothing. For a more permanent camp, you might want to devise a more comfortable seat. One possible design is easy to construct and surprisingly comfortable. Find three lengths of sturdy wood about two feet long and at least an inch and a half in diameter, lash these together to form a rigid equilateral triangle about 15 inches on a side, and support the seat at the apexes on large stones, fireplace logs or whatever else is available.

If that's still too crude for you, I have only one other suggestion. Buy one of those folding camp toilets having a plastic seat, folding legs and plastic bags to hang underneath. Remove the legs, leave the bags at home, and pack the seat in your backpack where it will be out of sight; flaunt it openly only if you are wholly immune to the guffaws of other hikers.

At this point we must talk about a problem that is painfully vexatious to those outdoor people who believe that anyone venturing into the great outdoors should be at least as civilized as an English butler. To put it bluntly, and hopefully not too crudely, every year thousands of people are polluting every place from ancient Indian ruins to natural cave shelters with their spoor. Why? Simply because they are either too ignorant and/or too lazy to dig a small hole in the ground. Without belaboring the point, each and every reader should vow to always bury his personal wastes because of health as well as aesthetic reasons. Also, take some pains to locate your improvised pit toilet so that it is downwind from the campsite, well away from traveled paths, and at least 200 feet from any still or running water.

Anyone old enough to have traveled the nation's trails two or three decades ago, and who still ventures onto them today, may, with good reason, be more than half convinced that an Orwellian future is in the making for generations of campers and hikers. If the hordes who now take to the woods in increasing numbers continue to litter the landscape as all too many already do, it may be necessary to set up check points through which all visitors to wilderness areas must pass when entering and leaving. At these stations all non-combustible and non-biodegradable materials carried by a hiker would be duly listed on a sheet which he would have to exhibit on leaving the area. Under threat of appropriate penalty, he would be forced to bring back all metal cans, plastic and glass bottles, and other items which obviously could not have been consumed.

Hopefully, the majority of hikers and campers can yet be educated to the realization that trash left lying along trails and in campsites are not only aesthetic horrors, but serious health hazards as well. Broken bottles and rusty cans can cause cuts that may become infected, especially because only basic first aid measures, at best, are available in these remote areas. Bottles, tin cans and even the folds of a discarded tarp can hold water that breeds mosquitoes that are, at the very least, annoying pests and, at the worst, carriers of serious diseases such as encephalitis.

Some unthinking campers harbor the notion that there's no harm in throwing food scraps around because they will either rot or be eaten by animals. But the fact is rotting food *stinks,* and draws flies which not only bite but can carry more diseases. Animals attracted to campsites by garbage can become nuisances or in some cases downright dangerous—especially in bear country. Even that cute raccoon family that has decided to make its burrow under a lean-to because of the good pickings can make life miserable for campers by passing on bloodsucking insects such as lice or fleas.

To help curb this very serious pollution problem, follow this simple *civilized* rule: If you can't eat it or safely burn it, bring it back out of the wilderness.

Incidentally, if you want to earn a gold star for your outdoor behavior, you will even avoid putting detergents into ponds, lakes and rivers when you wash dishes, clothes or yourself. Which brings us to another point. Just because you are alone in the wilderness most of the time, doesn't mean that you need to stay dirty. There's no tub or shower with hot running water, but a quick sponge bath can keep you clean. If you prefer to skip the baths, at least do other campers the favor of staying out of public shelters—sleep in your own tent or out in the open, preferably downwind, a couple hundred yards from neater folk.

A final word of advice is directed to those women who experience their "period" in the woods. Remember that there are no drug stores along wilderness trails, and that your cycle may shorten because of the unusual physical activity. Be especially careful about how you dispose of your sanitary needs, especially around camp, and even more so in bear country. It's impossible to really prove what goes on in the mind of a wild animal under any given circumstances, but one theory is that the two girls who were attacked and killed by a grizzly bear in Glacier National Park, Montana, in 1967, suffered their horrible fate because the bear smelled menstrual blood.

In this same context, a word about *hair* pollution. Ladies (and gentlemen), leave your hair spray at home when you go camping, especially in bear country. It has been pretty conclusively demonstrated that bears are attracted by the scents used in hair spray.

And consider this. Most wild animals a camper encounters in this country will not normally attack humans unless startled or provoked in some manner. But suppose that your natural *human* body odor is masked by cosmetics when a myopic bear or other hungry critter comes along. Dump all that scented beauty stuff out of your pack. You don't need it in the wilderness anyway; anyone truly in tune with the great out-of-doors emanates a glow that needs no artificial support.

18 First Aid

It seems that every spring some new type of kit comes on the market. What with snakebite kits, survival kits, sewing kits and water purification kits, it would seem that your pack only has room for kits.

I have never really found a kit that was worth half the asking price. They all seem to be just combinations of things that I normally carry. For example, I have constructed what I loosely call a first-aid kit, though many items are far from medicinal. It contains: aspirins, two Ace bandages (different sizes), water purification tablets, adhesive tape, bandages (Band-Aids), burn ointment, iodine, cotton swabs, needle, moleskin, thread, safety pins, a few buttons, tweezers, sunscreens, Alka Seltzer, throat lozenges, antacids (freeze-dried foods can be hell on your stomach after a few days), snakebite kit (although I'm not sure why I carry this) and sting relief spray.

With that list, it might seem that I don't have much room in my pack for anything else; but it really isn't that unwieldy. Since first-aid kits are as individual as the people who pack them, yours can be as light as you like. There are, however, several staples which should be part of anyone's kit.

Minor cuts are probably the most common injuries suffered by backpackers. If you accidentally slice a hand or finger with your knife or split a toe while chopping wood, you should immediately cleanse the wound with soap and water.

Next, cover the cut with a clean bandage; you could swab on some iodine if you don't mind the sting. Actually, this procedure isn't much different from what you'd do in your own bathroom. Once again, it's just a matter of common sense.

Minor burns are probably the second most frequent injury. Whether the burn is wet or dry, the treatment is the same: immediate immersion of the burned area into cold water. This should be kept up until the temperature of the burned area is reduced. Contrary to the tale of many old wives, under no circumstances should butter, grease or oil be applied to the burned area. Some sort of burn ointment is advisable, but only after complete sterilization and then used as a compress dressing.

The treatment of sprains is to place the injured ankle or wrist into ice-cold water and keep it there as long as possible. Continuous application of cold treatments is the best first-aid for sprains. Assuming it isn't a bad sprain and you can still walk on it, apply an Ace bandage around the injured area (even if it's your wrist). Check with your doctor for the proper method.

Splinters are a common hiker's malady. First, thoroughly wash the area around the sliver with soap and water; then try to remove the splinter as soon as possible to prevent infection.

Here's where the needle comes in. Sterilize over an open flame and allow to cool. Leave the soot on the needlepoint.

Some friends of mine advocate the use of prescription pain relievers such as Lomotil for bowels, Seconal for sleeping and antibiotics such as penicillin tablets or tetracycline for penicillin-sensitive people. Check with your doctor on the efficacy of any of these potent remedies.

Splints are a frequently needed item that can't be contained in any kit. You can improvise with tree limbs, blankets, even egg cartons; there *are* commercially packaged wire splints that could fit in your kit, but there wouldn't be room for anything else.

Of all the items found in a first-aid kit, there is one that can often spell the difference between a grim ordeal and an enjoyable encounter with the environment. It's called *moleskin,* and it prevents blisters. No backpacker should plan a trip of more than 1,000 yards without an adequate supply.

A lot of the other stuff is personal predilection. I happen to have fair skin, so I need plenty of sunscreens and lotions. I also take some zinc oxide, if hiking near the shore or under a hot sun, to block out virtually *all* the sun's rays. I'm not too enamored of bugs, either, and usually carry the large size of insect repellent. (By the way, some doctors prescribe Cutter's repellent combined with a sunscreen as the ultimate sun block.)

As I mentioned, it's pretty much individual preference combined with a large dosage of common sense.

Section III

19 Hiking In The Desert

To many hikers, the desert evokes images of sand dunes, mirages and the French Foreign Legion. It's seen as an inhospitable place supporting little life under a sweltering sun; to backpack in such a place would seem like madness. But to people who have experienced desert hiking, the picture is quite different. The desert becomes a place where wildlife and plants abound in startling variety and with audacious persistence. It's a land of many colors and changing climates—cold and hot, wet and dry. For the initiated, a desert backpacking trip can mean the finest in hiking experiences.

There are four distinct deserts in North America. The Great Basin Desert covers much of Nevada and Utah. It's a land of hot summers and cold winters, with its low annual precipitation spread fairly evenly throughout the year. The characteristic vegetation is sage-brush and saltbrush. South of this is the Mohave, occupying much of southeastern California. Here, what little moisture falls comes during the cool winters. Its summers boast some of the hottest temperatures on record. In large parts of southern California and Arizona is the Sonoran Desert with its winter and summer rainfalls which make it the "lushest" desert of the four. The Chihuahuan Desert spills into the U.S. from Mexico; it covers parts of New Mexico and Texas with its spiny shrubs and cacti. Taken together, these four desert areas comprise about five percent of the land area of North America. The figure seems low until you consider that it means half a million square miles of backpacking possibilities.

For most of us, desert and heat are synonymous. Although this is not always accurate, coping with the heat is a definite concern whenever it comes to the matter of desert hiking. Heat, however, is relative. My "hot" may be your "pleasant." Much of the way we feel at different temperatures depends on individual metabolism, physical conditioning and climatic conditioning. In the long run, however, one of the most important factors in preparing your body for the rigors of desert hiking is acclimation.

If you live near the desert and are used to getting exercise in its heat, your body probably has already adjusted itself to the climate. A person coming from Wyoming for an April backpacking trip in Arizona has some adjusting to do. In this case, three or four days of acclimation starting with a short hour-long hike the first day and increasing the length of the shakedown hikes on the following days would be a good way to ease into a longer backpacking trip.

When it comes to your clothing, there are three different theories of ways to keep cool. The first one uses the "when it's cold, put things on; when it's hot, take things off" reasoning. This theory has some merit in other regions, but when the desert sun is blazing, a hiker wearing nothing but shorts and boots is asking for trouble. First, there is the problem of sunburn, which can come on in a hurry in the clear air of the desert atmosphere. More important, though, is the fact that exposed skin absorbs heat faster than it does when covered with the proper clothing. So although stripping down in the desert may seem sensible, it can lead to deep-fried skin and dangerous overheating.

Covering up makes more sense when hiking in the hot sun. It not only provides shade for your skin, it also helps protect you against the spiny onslaught of prickly plants typical of arid regions.

The kind of clothing you use is important. Light colored cloths are most effective in reflecting the sun. Cotton is the best bet because many of the synthetic materials, even when light in color, heat up too quickly in sunlight. In addition to covering up with long pants and a long sleeved shirt, protect your head with a light colored hat that has vent holes in the crown. Since most wide brimmed hats are impractical to wear when carrying a high riding frame pack, you'll also want to protect your neck with a bandana. Or you can attach a piece of cloth to the back of your hat in the best Foreign Legion tradition.

A final concept in keeping cool is to get wet. Now this idea has obvious drawbacks in the desert where having enough water is often your greatest concern. However, where water is plentiful—the Colorado and the Rio Grande flow through the heart of desert country—dousing your clothing with water is indeed a way of keeping cool. As water on wet clothes evaporates, it will have a cooling effect on your body. In addition, it reduces the amount of sweating your body has to maintain in order to cool itself. Therefore, it conserves your body fluids. Actually, getting wet is merely an extension of the cover up theory, since your clothes are needed to hold the moisture next to your skin. Water thrown directly on exposed skin rolls off too fast to be of long lasting help.

One area of clothing that is particularly important in beating the heat but is often given little consideration is footwear. Ground temperatures in the desert heat may be 40 to 50 degrees higher than the air temperature in the shade. For example, National Park Service employees in Death Valley recorded an amazing 201 degrees ground temperature in 1972. That kind of reading is an exception, but it still underlines the need for footwear that will insulate your feet from the hot ground. Boots with heavy lugged soles are good; the farther apart the lugs the cooler your feet will be. Mid soles will add more insulation, and woven plastic insoles provide air circulation. In addition, heavy socks changed often, and the liberal use of foot powder, provide protection against both heat and blisters.

Although the proper clothing goes a long way in helping the desert backpacker cope with the heat, there are other ways of maintaining comfort. When midday temperatures are expected to be extremely warm, hiking in the early morning or the evening is a good practice. The morning is the best time, because the ground has had the entire night to cool off. In the evening, the sun may be low or even down, but heat will still radiate from the ground. Hiking in the middle of the night, when there is only moonlight to illuminate the surroundings, can be one of the most exhilarating desert experiences. The air is cool, and the moonlight creates a softening atmosphere to the often harsh seeming environment. Also, this is the only time when you get a chance to see the nocturnal plants and animals of the desert such as the Nightblooming Cereus, the Kit and Gray Fox. Night hiking does require some precautions, however. It's advisable to carry a flashlight to check out those poorly lighted spots where old mine shafts might lurk or where you might get jabbed with cholla or prickly pear stickers.

During the hottest part of the day, it is usually smart to take a cue from the desert creatures; find a place off the ground in the shade and sit out the heat. When natural shade isn't available, a poncho or ground cloth should be rigged to give you shade along with plenty of ventilation. Although a tent may be handy at night, it's usually turned into an oven during the day because of insufficient air circulation.

The sun, however, is not the only source of heat when hiking in the desert. Consider your kitchen. Many backpackers depend on a backpacking stove instead of a cooking fire to prepare their meals. A stove and fuel adds more weight to your pack, weight that might be utilized for carrying extra water. In addition, backpacking stoves of the self-pressurized variety have the annoying habit of "flaming out" through their pressure release valves when they get overheated. The problem with a cooking fire, on the other hand, is the difficulty of finding suitable fuel in some desert areas. Desert country is certainly not devoid of fuel; many green, pulpy looking plants have internal, woody skeletons that make suitable firewood when dry. But finding enough of this fuel isn't always easy. In the long run, the nature of the particular desert country you plan to walk through, and the limitations you'll have to put on weight, will determine whether you should plan on cooking over a fire or a stove.

There is no doubt that, under normal conditions, your biggest concern in desert backpacking will be water. Not only is water difficult to find, it's also extremely important in maintaining your body's cooling system while hiking in the heat of a desert climate. Sweating is the way you get rid of excess heat from your body in order to maintain an internal temperature of around 99 degrees. It is possible to lose a pint of water an hour through sweating if you are hiking in the desert heat. This water along with salt has to be replaced or your cooling mechanism may cease to function, resulting in heat stroke. Heat cramps and heat exhaustion may also result from excessive loss of body water and salt.

Individual water needs will vary from person to person, but a gallon a day per person should be a minimum when backpacking in the desert. Under really hot conditions you might need two gallons a day per person. The important thing is that you not be Spartan. You should drink regularly even when you don't feel particularly thirsty and even when you don't appear to be sweating a great deal. Sweat evaporates quickly in the low humidity of the desert, often before it has time to form noticeable beads on your skin. You should also put extra salt on your food and occasionally take salt tablets.

All this water, of course, means a lot of extra bulk and weight that you're probably going to have to carry yourself. Deserts are notorious for their unreliable watering holes. Even when creeks and springs are indicated on a map, check with someone who has been in the area recently to make sure you can depend on these water supplies. If you do have to carry your own water, it's going to mean 8⅓ pounds for every gallon. Even when you're able to get by with only a light sleeping bag and no tent, the weight of water will soon limit the length of your trip. And remember, when your water is half gone, your trip should be half over.

Carrying your water requires some logistics. There's the matter of containers. You'll want water bottles that won't leak and are resistant to splitting and punctures. Wide mouthed, quart-sized plastic containers work well because they are light, easy to fill and can be distributed throughout your pack to provide proper balance. For the most carrying ease, you should try to keep full water containers as high and as close to your back as possible.

When there is the possibility of finding water along your route, you should know where to look for it. Springs and creeks will be marked on maps, but there are other possibilities. In rocky areas, rainfall is often caught in holes and depressions that are sunk in the rocks. If these natural water containers are shaded from the sun, water trapped in these potholes may not evaporate for many days. Even dry looking stream beds may harbor water in holes under the downstream side of large rocks.

Despite stories to the contrary, do not depend on getting sufficient water for your needs by cutting open barrel cactus or by making solar stills. What water these methods might produce would hardly be enough to keep you going.

A final possibility for solving your desert water problem is to make water caches along your planned route of travel. These resupply points have to be well thought out ahead of time so they'll

Fresh water in a rock pothole *(Linda Curtis)*

syncronize with your water needs. In addition, you may have to spend some time hiking the water supply in so it will be in convenient spots along your route. It is one sure way of allowing you to make lengthy backpacking trips that might otherwise be impossible.

The desert has many moods, however; during certain times of year, water may become a problem of a different kind—flash floods. Most desert soil absorbs water very slowly, and most desert rains come in the form of torrential cloud bursts. The combination makes for the transformation of a "dry wash" into a wall of brown, roiling water within minutes. If you happen to be hiking in the "dry wash" when this downpour occurs, you're in for big trouble. The matter is further complicated by the fact that a flash flood may occur in areas that haven't even received any rain. A storm miles away may dump enough moisture to fill natural drainages with flood waters that won't dissipate until long after they've gone beyond the area hit by the storm.

Cold hiking in the Sonoran Desert *(Linda Curtis)*

Hiking the canyon country of the Great Basin Desert *(Linda Curtis)*

Because of the very real possibility of flash floods during the desert's rainy season, you should be particularly careful where you hike and where you make your camp. Avoid walking through narrow, steep walled canyons when you think it might rain. When you are forced to hike through such canyons, carry a topographic map of the area; you can figure how long it will take to get through, and you can plan possible escape routes. Where afternoon thunder showers are the rule, plan to hike through flood areas in the morning. Wisely select your campsite. Make sure you are not in any natural drainage area, and camp well above the high water mark of any flowing or intermittent stream. Also keep all members of your party on the same side of a possible flood area. I know of a group that was divided for two days by the waters of a raging desert stream. They had to sit it out in their own separate camps until the water was low enough to cross safely and they could continue their hike together.

If the possibility of too much water is one of the ironies of desert hiking, so is the possibility of being cold. The fact is that winter in the desert may mean warm days and frosty nights. In the high deserts, it could easily mean snow. There are also those times when your hike starts in the desert and ends in the mountains, where an entirely different climate and life zone exists. When backpacking in the Sonoran Desert, you frequently encounter this sort of situation.

Obviously, planning for this kind of trip calls for some special considerations. You've got to take clothing that will be suitable for a wide range of temperatures. You've also got to plan on the possibility of finding no water but hope that you'll run across the occasional pocket of snow or pothole of water.

Despite the special considerations that go into backpacking in the desert, it can offer some of the most intriguing kinds of hiking opportunities found anywhere. Probably nowhere else are the possibilities of archeological discovery quite so rich—whether it be in finding a remote cliff dwelling in a canyon of the Great Basin Desert or stumbling upon pot shards in the Chihuahuan Desert. For bird watchers, wildflower lovers, photographers or any backpackers interested in remote and varied hiking, the desert's many moods will constantly amaze and reward you.

Mountain hiking means coping with the ups and downs of the environment.

20 Mountain Backpacking

Mountains mean different things to different people. The Colorado backpacker looks at the rolling contours of a Vermont mountain and sees only foothills, while the hiker from Florida is awe-inspired by Colorado peaks considered molehills by Montanans. Whether looked at as mountains or molehills, however, there is one thing that never changes—a thousand foot increase in elevation means uphill hiking whether you start at sea level or 6,000 feet. And then, of course, you've heard the old adage about what goes up. The down part applies to backpacking as well. Mountain hiking means coping with these ups and downs.

Before you ever set foot on a mountain trail, you should set foot into a properly fitting pair of medium-weight hiking boots. You might be able to get away with less when backpacking at sea level, but mountain terrain requires a boot with plenty of support. You needn't overboard, however. You'll need a hiking boot, not a *climbing* boot. Climbing boots may make you look rugged, but they'll wear you out on the trail because they're too heavy and stiff.

For the average adult, a pair of hiking boots should weigh between three and five pounds. They should have lugged soles and some degree of arch support. Interior padding at the heel and ankle is important; it helps keep your foot from sliding up and down in the boot—a likely tendency when hiking up mountains. The importance of a properly fitting pair of hiking boots can't be emphasized enough. By settling for anything less, you are almost assured of a miserable trip or one that will end abruptly.

Once you have the right boots, it's important to know how to hike with them in the mountains. That may sound ridiculous, but there is a basic rhythm involved in good hiking that should be maintained when the going gets steep. On level ground we often fall into a particular pace and speed. We can sustain that hiking rhythm without stopping for long periods of time. Where most of us falter is on the up and downhill stretches. Going uphill, the tendency is to break into an irregular stride and speed, stopping for rests frequently. This destroys any semblance of rhythm and makes progress more tiring physically as well as psychologically.

In order to get in a groove when you hit the steep stuff, begin by shortening your stride and slowing your pace, but try to keep that sense of rhythm in your movement. Where the trail becomes irregular and you're forced to alter your stride, take two short steps in place of a long one—as if you are keeping time. Often it helps to synchronize each breath you take with a given number of steps. After you've done this consciously for awhile, the built-in rhythm of this kind of pacing will take over, and you won't have to think about it. The point is that the backpacker with a slow but steady pace will always surpass the hare who ascends in fits and starts.

There are a few other hiking tricks you can use when the going gets really rough or when you are traveling cross country and have to select your own route. On extreme grades, even when you are hiking with a slow rhythmic pace, your leg muscles are greatly strained. You can give them a momentary rest during each step by using what is called the lock step. As you straighten out your leg at the end of each step, lock it in the straight position for a moment. Most of the weight of your body and pack is then supported by your *bones* and not your muscles. The lock step should not be exaggerated or it becomes halting. Instead, make just a slight pause with your leg in the locked position. You'll be surprised at how the momentary rest of your muscles will enable you to keep climbing.

Cross-country travel in the mountains poses some other problems. To make going easier on the upgrades you should either make long traverses across the face of the hill or make a series of zig-zag switchbacks. Both of these techniques will increase the distance you have to travel, but they make the hiking much less strenuous.

Mountain backpacking often requires crossing scree—the broken and loose rocks at the bottom of a cliff or headwall. Because these rocks have a tendency to tip and slide, be especially careful with your footing in such areas. Test footholds before putting your full weight on them, and avoid leaping from rock to rock. Try not to hike directly below or above another backpacker as falling rocks can be a real hazard.

When it comes to hiking *down* mountains most people think it must be easier than hiking up. It probably is on the lungs. But the legs, knees and feet take just as much punishment going down as going up. Gravity and momentum make it necessary for you to apply the brakes while descending. This means your muscles have to be used constantly to hold your body back. Your knees are subjected to constant jarring, and your feet are crammed forward in your boots. To lessen the strain, you should try to maintain the same kind of rhythm you do when going up steep pitches. It's particularly important to take short steps. A lot of short steps when going down are much easier on your legs than a fewer number of long steps.

This far the focus has been on hiking problems that you might encounter in any highlands. However, when you start heading for those rarefied peaks, you have some very special considerations. The first one is the matter of acclimation.

The backpacker with a slow but steady pace will always surpass the one who ascends in fits and starts.

When you head up into the rarefied atmosphere, there are special considerations—such as acclimation.

Almost everyone has some reaction to elevations above 10,000 feet. It may only be a feeling of fatigue or it may be a full blown case of mountain sickness which brings on headaches, weakness, nausea and insomnia. To give your body time to acclimate, try to spend two or three days at fairly high elevations before doing any serious hiking. Because there is a decrease in the oxygen supply as you increase in altitude, your body has to make adjustments before it can function well. The biggest change comes with an increase in the production of red blood corpuscles for the extra hemoglobin needed to carry more oxygen through your body. Most of that increased production takes place in the first three days but continues to some degree even after that.

When you do start to hike at elevations over 10,000 feet, there are still things you can do to help your body cope with the situation. Slow your normal pace. You'll probably feel the necessity of this. Even if you feel fine, don't take the chance of becoming overly fatigued at these high elevations. Also, avoid eating large meals. Instead, have light snacks throughout the day. This will greatly reduce the diversion of blood to the digestive system and free it for the job of supplying you with oxygen.

You should find that light eating is no problem; many hikers experience a loss of appetite, especially for fats and proteins, at high altitudes. However, it is important to keep your body supplied with fuel to heat it and to maintain its energy. Only experience will tell you what kind of food you may find distasteful at high altitudes, and even then your tastes may change. The best thing to do is carry as large a variety of food as is practical. Some hikers find that antacid tablets relieve minor stomach problems. If that fails and you can't face food of any kind, get off the mountain.

Another thing that happens to you at high elevations is an increase in your loss of fluids. With the increase in your breathing, more moisture is leaked from your body through expiration. In addition, sweat evaporates from your body more rapidly in the dry, windy air of the mountains; this makes you feel as if you're hardly sweating at all. Without a continual replacement of this fluid, you'll become dehydrated. Drink plenty of liquids and take salt tablets.

Almost any mountain, regardless of its elevation, is more exposed to the elements than the lowlands. In fact, mountains have a way of creating their own weather. Therefore, when you are on the summit or the side of one, you have to be prepared for extremes. I have started out on many a summer mountain trip in shirt sleeves and ended up needing clothing for wind, rain and cold.

Mountain hiking can mean more exposure to the sun. Wear a long sleeved shirt, long pants, and use sun block.

If you are forced to camp on a slope, sleep with your head uphill.

Before starting up any mountain, you should know the possible extremes to expect for that particular time of year. The weather on Washington's Mt. Rainier is going to have quite a different June climate than Mt. Ajo in Arizona during the same time. Check guide books or talk with local hikers to learn what to expect.

During most summer months, however, you'll want to pack along a wool long-sleeved shirt, a wool sweater, a combination rain/wind parka and perhaps even wind pants. Wool hat and mittens will help complete your compleat mountain wardrobe.

When most hikers think of exposure to extreme mountain weather conditions, they think of the obvious. Yet pleasant, sunny weather can also be extreme. The sun is much more potent at high elevations because ultraviolet rays are stronger in the thin atmosphere. Most suntan lotions are not sufficient protection. Sun screens or blocks are your best bet. Again, zinc oxide is recommended. Apply the stuff liberally, and wear a long-sleeved shirt and a hat.

Mountains in the summer are more likely to generate afternoon electrical storms, and hikers in high places are vulnerable to lightning strikes. When a storm starts to brew, you should get off summits and exposed ridges. If you end up in the heart of a storm, get away from metal objects (like packframes) and hunker down on some insulator (such as a sleeping pad). Backpackers seeking shelter in caves are seeking trouble. Nearby lightning strikes have a tendency to arc across the entrance.

Some sort of shelter *is* needed when you plan to spend more than a day in the mountains. Protection against strong winds and rain is best found in a good mountain tent. A-frame tents seem to stand up to wind better than other designs because the tent and the rainfly can be pitched very taut. Actually, the whole process of selecting a good campsite and pitching your tent properly is the key to spending a comfortable night in the mountains even when the weather is extreme. Finding a level piece of ground may be difficult. But at least avoid humps or depressions which would put the two ends of your tent on different planes. If you do have to camp on a slope, you'll want to sleep with your head uphill. Ideally, your camp should have an eastern exposure, which will offer some protection from prevailing west winds and give you a little early morning sunlight to dry things off.

If you have to pitch a tent in the wind, pitch it with one end *into* the wind. Stake those two corners first, then unroll the rest of the tent and stake the other two corners. You'll find that steel skewers work best in really rocky soil, or you can use the rocks themselves to

You may have to rely on snow banks for your water supply. *(Linda Curtis)*

anchor guy lines. The important thing is to pitch the tent as taut as possible, so it won't flap in the wind.

Another important campsite concern is water, and it isn't always that easy to find in the mountains. I once took a five-day hike along the Gallatin divide in southwestern Montana. We were above timberline the entire time and above streams and lakes for three days. During that period we had to rely on old snowbanks for our water. Being above timberline meant packing a stove and carrying about twice as much fuel as usual in order to melt the snow.

Stoves are often a necessity when backpacking in the mountains, since firewood is either scarce or simply not available. Besides, a stove is a good piece of safety equipment. On a cold, rainy day, you can use it to prepare a hot trail lunch. There are times when hot food might be more than a luxury; it could be *imperative*.

Cold damp weather, particularly when it's windy and you're tired and hungry, can easily produce hypothermia. (See Chapter 12.)

Although hypothermia is a possibility inherent in mountain backpacking, proper food, clothing and shelter will go a long way toward preventing it. It's certainly no reason to stay out of high places. Besides, the air is always clearer—even when you're in the clouds. Wildflowers seem more vibrant, and the views are obviously more panoramic. It's definitely worth all the ups and downs.

Mountain country has attractions that keep you coming back.

21 Coastlines

Hiking along America's coasts is unlike any other experience on foot. The trail is often an ocean beach pounded by waves on sand. Gulls and salt air replace eagles and alpine cool. The view is different. The terrain underfoot is different. And the dangers are different.

But the basic principles of hiking and backpacking remain the same. The more you know about where you are going and what you're going to do when you get there, the better chance you have of having a fruitful and enjoyable trip. In coastal trekking, you can prepare for tides; for rain forest climates that drop 140 inches of annual precipitation; for heat or cold; and for the wherever-you-go, in-the-bush regret that you left a piece of specialized equipment behind. You can even bone up on your natural history so you know which birds are chasing the waves and which are looking for fish.

Not until a person reaches the coast, however, does he truly begin to feel the power and beauty of its unique rhythms. The most perceptible rhythm is the rising and falling of tides.

Tides result from the gravitational pull of the moon and sun, which causes ocean waters to bulge on both sides of the earth. As the earth rotates beneath the bulges, water levels alternately rise and fall along coastlines. Twice a month, the sun and moon lie in a direct line with the earth causing exceptionally large tides known as spring tides. When the sun and moon lie at right angles to the earth, also twice a month, the sun weakens the moon's gravitational pull, resulting in relatively small tides known as neap tides.

Tides, however, are more complicated than the result of shifting solar and lunar bodies. The contours of a coastline and its relation to the ocean basin beyond often modifies the tide's effect in a particular area.

Most tides along North America, especially along the Atlantic—from Nova Scotia to Florida—occur twice a day, peaking every 12 hours and 25 minutes. The Pacific coast tides also rise and fall twice daily but not as regularly as Atlantic tides. The same is true of western Florida and the eastern half of the Gulf of Mexico. Near the Mississippi delta and along the coast of Texas, tides occur only once a day.

How high does a tide rise? It depends on where you are. The maximum difference between low and high tide in Nova Scotia is 5.9 feet; in Oregon 10.8 feet; and along California 12.8 feet. The tide might rise only a foot at Key West, Florida, but it can rise up to 50 feet along the long, narrow Bay of Fundy on the east coast of Canada.

Most tides, however, are predictable enough so that tidetables giving clock times can be made of their ups and downs. Wherever a person hikes along the ocean, it is advisable to study a copy of the area's tidetable. Tidetables are often available at seashore trailheads and park headquarters. Failure to study a tidetable can result in discomfort, even death.

Take Scott's Bluff, for example. This rocky headland, or promontory, juts out into the Pacific Ocean along the preserved wilderness beach of Olympic National Park in Washington. Reaching Scott's Bluff at high tide often means a hiker must take a headland trail up a mudslide into rain forest terrain. A hiker reaching Scott's Bluff at low or medium tide can quickly and easily walk around, rather than over, the headland.

Taylor Point, a mile north of Scott's Bluff, is different. It is one of four points between LaPush and Oil City that cannot be rounded *even at low tide*. Ignorant and lazy hikers have tried to round Taylor Point at low tide, only to find their route blocked by rock and rising water. Unable to turn around, because of rising water behind them and unable to climb sheer rock, they were eventually washed to their deaths in the sea.

Then, what *does* a person do during high tide? He takes headland trails that detour up and over impassable promontories. He hikes wide beaches where upper reaches escape the force of up to two tons per square inch of breaking waves. He watches waves toss trunks of driftwood larger than most living trees in the Midwest. He eats. He dries wet clothes near driftwood fires. He chats with fellow hikers. But most of the time he just listens to the roar of waves pounding sand and rock. The ocean's sound is overwhelming. The rest is mainly silence.

I could count on one hand the number of places along the Atlantic, Pacific and Gulf coasts where a backpacker could feel at home: Point Reyes National Seashore in California; Cape Hatteras National Seashore in North Carolina; Olympic National Park in Washington; Oregon Dunes National Recreation Area. There are

Scene at Ruby Beach, Olympic National Park *(National Park Service, Olympic National Park, Port Angeles, Washington)*

195

other national seashores and recreation areas along America's coasts where the public can meander and hike, but not for serious backpacking. We're back to the one hand.

Acadia National Park, along the coast of Maine, helps prove the point. Although there are many miles of trails ranging from easy to rugged, backpacking isn't allowed. It's come in a car or camp by a car.

Everglades National Park in Florida has only one area accessible to backcountry hikers; most of the other designated beach campsites are accessible only by boat. Redwood National Park, in northern California—including its nearby redwoods state parks—has only one eight-mile trail open to backpackers.

The situation is depressingly clear. Of the thousands of miles of American coasts, a scant 200 to 300 miles is open to you and me. Certainly, there are state parks and national wildlife refuges along our coasts open to hiking. But except for such areas as Point Reyes and Olympic National Park, most places favor day-hiking over serious treks.

Like hiking in the mountains, where a hiker expects to accommodate himself to thinner, cooler temperatures, coastal hiking usually implies a change of climate. This is especially true for people who journey from America's interior to hike its coastlines.

Generally, coasts are cooler and wetter than inland areas, depending upon the season. Winters along the Middle and North Atlantic Lowlands Region are somewhat warmer near the coast than farther inland. The warmer waters of the Atlantic furnish heat to the lower layers of the atmosphere. However, summers along the same seacoast are cooler than those of the inland lowlands.

The Pacific Coast, ranging from mid-California north to Canada, remains cool during the summer. It also remains wet. The west side of the mountains of the Pacific Northwest has a rain forest climate. Olympic National Park's preserved wilderness beach gets about 140 inches of annual precipitation, 76 percent of it falling between October and March, or 16 inches a month during winter. People out there say if you're going to wait for the sun before visiting the coast, well . . . you might never visit the coast.

The same is true of Oregon Dunes National Recreation Area and California's Del Norte Coast Redwoods State Park; they receive 80

Hiking near Muldrow Glacier in Alaska.

inches and 110 inches of rainfall a year respectively. Compare that to Minnesota's annual precipitation of 35 inches. Florida's Everglades doesn't get its rain until summer, and then a hiker should expect spotty precipitation every day.

Rain doesn't have to ruin a hike. Just the opposite. If properly equipped, a hiker can not only walk through any squall, he can enjoy himself while doing it.

Sufficient rain gear includes more than a good rain garment. Tent flies are absolutely essential to keep a tent and its occupants dry. Rubber boots are frequently used to replace leather boots in wet climates, although leather boots that are properly oiled can hold off moisture for days. Rain chaps, too, make comfortable additions to anyone's rain gear.

When you get right down to it, hiking in the rain along the ocean is no different from hiking in rain anywhere. You need to stay warm and/or dry. From fall through winter to spring, being wet or cold invites hypothermia. The insulating qualities of clothing and gear become more critical.

A summer alternative to rain gear while hiking coastlines is to strip to shorts and hike near-naked in the rain. (Here, women backpackers may use their discretion.) The exertion of carrying a pack will warm the body. When you stop and begin to cool, just towel off, don warm clothes, and put on a poncho or jacket. Again, be wary of hypothermia symptoms. (See Chapter 12.)

Any coastline hiker who consistently hikes in a wet climate should seriously evaluate whether his sleeping bag should be insulated with polyester fiberfill or goose down. Goose down is useless when wet, but some of the new synthetic fiberfills insulate *even when wet.* Similarly, wet cotton is useless as an insulator, while the opposite is true of wool. In cold coastal temperatures, from 20 to 40 degrees Fahrenheit, a tossel cap will help the body preserve a large amount of heat. So will gloves.

Enough words of wetdom. All coasts are not cool and damp. We need only think of Florida's coasts, the coasts of the Gulf of Mexico, Mexico's Pacific coasts, and Massachusetts' Cape Cod in summer.

A surfside backpacker probably has more to fear from the sun than anything else. The sun's ultraviolet rays are reflected and refracted by sand and water, exposing skin to light intensity it probably isn't accustomed to. Even people who normally tan easily can become seriously sunburned while hiking along seashores. My advice to hot coast hikers is to wear hats, sunglasses and to protect supersensitive skin by coating it with zinc oxide. As is customary in any hotspot, the length of daily exposure to the sun should be increased gradually from day to day, thus avoiding such niceties as gut aches, blistering shoulders and heat stroke.

Despite the infinite, tantalizing amounts of water pounding and bordering every ocean beach, you can't drink it. Salt water increases, not quenches, thirst. It's not like the refreshing image in the iced tea commercial—of a thirsty man falling backwards into a cool swimming pool. It's more like the shipwrecked survivor floating at sea in a rubber raft under a hot sun paraphrasing Mr. Coleridge: "Water, water, everywhere, but not a drop to drink!"

A long hike along the seashore should receive the same serious preparation that precedes any lengthy excursion. Like any plant or animal, the human body requires water to function, up to one gallon per person per day under hot and strenuous circumstances. Our bodies exude sweat, which evaporates, cooling the body in return.

Profuse perspiration, such as when backpacking with 30 to 40 pounds on a sandy beach under a hot sun, drains the body of valuable fluids and salt. If this fluid and salt is not replaced, sickness occurs. How sick a hiker gets depends on how much water and salt is dispelled. Avoiding illness from lack of water is a simple matter of carrying sufficient water in plastic jugs, canteens, water bags, flasks or knowing places enroute to one's destination where fresh water can be secured. Ingesting prescribed amounts of salt tablets fights salt loss. A hiker can also mix one or two teaspoons of table salt in a quart or half gallon of water, marking the jug to distinguish it from unsalted water. Periodic swigs of salty water at sensible intervals between fresh water drinks will keep salt loss adequately under control.

Unfortunately, seacoasts have their healthy share of bugs. Park brochures from Florida's Everglades National Park insist that an insect repellent is necessary for bearable hiking during wet, summer months. Acadia National Park in Maine warns of common insects in May, June and July—as do most coastal areas. Vicious blackflies are indigenous to hot beaches, while tidal flats encourage an abundance of mosquitoes. Woodticks seem to be more prevalent in late spring and early summer wherever there is grass and woodland. A hiker's only defenses against such voracious insects remain the perennial standbys: insect repellents, clothing over exposed skin, and fast hands.

Once packed and at a seacoast, a hiker is on his own. A unique hiking environment is all around. The hiker hears the crash of surf, perhaps the earth's most ancient and perennial sound. His trail consists of shifting sands, trunks of driftwood, inland trails, rocky headlands, screaming gulls and more sand. In coastline rain forests, the wide-eyed hiker sees mosses exude droplets of water; he sees sunlight through giant redwoods, alders and hemlock forests. On sunny beaches, he feels the sand underfoot vibrate as blue swells collapse into white spray. His nose picks up new scents. His eyes spy colorful starfish, shells, ubiquitous anemones and the incessant sandpipers that probe the sand for mole crabs. All senses are alive. Hiking along a seacoast is not only an experience unto itself. It has a strange way of making a hiker feel closer to *home*.

Internal frame packs are recommended for forest trekking—less likely than external frames to grab at every branch.

22 *Woods*

Since I was brought up in the East, whenever I think of *woods,* deep woods, I think of those forested expanses in Maine where secluded lakes are stocked with fat, jumping fish and where small black flies are forever attacking humans. In my mind's eye that will always be the Forest Primeval. Obviously there are other kinds of woods—the rolling forests of upstate New York and Massachusetts, the vast, flat tracts of woods in Minnesota, dense stands of lodgepole timber in the Rockies and the lush rain forests of the Pacific Northwest. They all have their own kind of allure, and they all require certain kinds of backpacking know-how when it comes to hiking and camping under their branches.

The one thing that all forests have in common is the fact that they enclose you. There may be the occasional meadow or ridgeline outcropping that will let you see the forest for the trees, but most of the time the trees will surround you. This state of affairs poses no problems when you are traveling on well marked and well maintained trails. Head off on your own, however, and you've got to find a way of keeping track of yourself. And the best way of doing it is through the use of topographical maps and a compass. (See Chapter 14.)

Topo maps show you what the surrounding area is like even when you can't see more than a few dozen yards through the trees. In addition to presenting the contour of the land, they indicate forested areas, clearings and water courses along with man made objects such as roads and buildings.

Hiking through the woods while looking at a compass can be compared to driving in rush hour traffic while reading a newspaper. In both cases, collision with something is almost a certainty. To avoid this problem in the woods, you should use landmarks. When you have ascertained your line of travel on the compass, set your sight on some prominent tree, stump or snag that falls along the path of that line. You can then walk to the object without looking at your compass. When you have reached the landmark, sight in on another one with the use of your compass. Continue this process until you have reached your destination.

There will be times, of course, when something will get in the way of your straight line of travel—a lake or a rock outcropping, perhaps. If you can see beyond the obstacle to your landmark, just skirt the barrier and continue to the landmark. In the case where a barrier obscures your view, you'll have to use other tactics. The best method is to turn at right angles to your line of travel and walk, counting the paces, until you have cleared the obstacle. Then turn another right angle, walking until you're beyond the barrier. Finally, make a third 90 degree turn, and return the same number of paces you took on the way out. You will then be at a point where you can refer again to your direction of travel arrow and establish another landmark.

As important as a map and compass are in keeping track of yourself in any forest, there are times when a more circuitous and exploratory kind of travel is more interesting. This is where game trail hiking can really become addictive.

Go into any deep woods where there's a decent population of deer or elk, and you'll run into their trails. The trails may seem to wander, but they all have a purpose for the animals. They'll lead to and from wintering and summering grounds. These will be long distance trails and usually go from low to high country. In a more localized area, the trails will lead to watering holes, feeding grounds and escape cover.

If you aren't too particular about where you're going, following game trails will give you a good sense of the area and should give you some interesting trails to follow. In forests with heavy under-growth, there'll be times when your only way through will be on these natural trails. More than once I've followed the paths of deer and elk through woodlands that would otherwise have been impenetrable.

Whether following game trails or just bushwhacking or even when hiking on established trails with low hanging branches, a typical framepack can be a contrivance of the devil when backpacking in the woods. The high profile of the frame, which is one of the reasons for the effectiveness of these packs, makes it a perfect branch snagger. Twist and bend as you might, that overhead baggage will catch, bump and bash into any part of the forest that comes near your head.

For day trips, the use of a small or medium rucksack is a simple solution. But for longer trips in the woods, where you'll have to carry 20 to 30 pounds of gear, a large soft pack or one with an interior frame is recommended.

It used to be that even moderately heavy loads with an old rucksack were real torture. But modern makers of soft packs have come up with bag shapes that fit the contour of your back and hips when they're loaded. Another possibility is the use of internal frame packs. They are made with either flat stays in H, X and Y configurations or with molded semi-ridged foam. None of these are quite as efficient as the external pack frames, but they won't grab at every branch in the forest either.

Another item of equipment you might want to consider is a pair of "bush" pants. In heavy undergrowth, regular pants offer little protection from bushes and briars. Pants made of a heavy duty duck cloth, however, are highly resistant to tears and are more effective against the painful sting of backlashing branches. They're also quite water repellent, which makes them doubly helpful when the undergrowth is wet.

Wet forests. Rain forests. Whatever name you use, they call for some special considerations. Your boots should be the primary concern. Whether a forest floor is muddy, marshy or just plain soggy, it can soak through a pair of "waterproofed" leather hiking boots in no time. When it comes to wet woods, you're better off wearing a combination rubber/leather boot or an all rubber boot. The traditional Maine hunting boot, with its rubber bottom and leather upper, has long been a favorite of hikers venturing into damp forests. The rubber bottom protects you in water up to several inches deep, yet internal moisture has a chance to escape through the breathable uppers. When you get into really wet spots, all-rubber boots are the answer. Your feet may get wet from perspiration and condensation but not nearly as wet as they would without water-proof protection.

Raingear is a second consideration. Forests have a habit of showering rain upon you long after the downpour has ended, particularly when there's a wind blowing. Ponchos that fit over you and your pack, a favorite of wet weather hikers, are anathema in the deep woods because they latch onto twigs and branches too readily. Fully waterproof rain suits are hardly suitable because you sweat too much in them when hiking. The best bet, although not completely satisfactory, is a highly water repellent rain parka that is still breathable. It will let inner moisture out even though it may allow some outer moisture in. The parka can be worn in conjunction with rain chaps or water repellent "bush" pants.

The last big item for a trip into the heart of a damp forest is insect repellent. Take along *plenty*.

The specific problems of hiking in the woods usually have to do with tree- and brush- related things. Branch backlash is a real annoyance when hiking behind someone else, and it can be dangerous—especially if you get struck in the eye. To minimize the problem, hold limbs and branches until the person in back of you can grab onto them, or make sure he stays far enough behind to avoid being hit by a released branch.

Downfalls pose another problem. Fallen saplings and small sized trees often cross your path even on established trails. If the downfalls are low enough to the ground, the temptation is to step on them in passing. When the wood is damp, a nasty fall is a real possibility. I've been ignominiously dumped on the ground enough times to recommend stepping *over* these downfalls instead of on them.

An abundance of trees can pose several problems when it comes to setting up camp. There's usually no difficulty in finding enough room to set up your tent or tarp (unless you're into deeper woods

Step *over* fallen trees. If the wood is damp, you can be in for a nasty spill.

than you ought to be), and trunks and limbs often act as convenient guy line anchors. However, you should carefully check out the trees you plan to camp beneath. Be sure to avoid dead trees or trees with dead branches. A wind could send both branches and trees crashing into your shelter. I've seen it happen, luckily, to an empty tent. Also avoid camping among trees that are higher than the surrounding forest or that are on a prominent ridge or summit. Lightning is attracted to these high points. The annals of backpacking history are filled with tales of campers being zapped while camped in just such a spot.

Of all the things you'd think you'd be least likely to worry about while backpacking in the woods, it would probably be fuel gathering. Think again. For starters, there are many national parks and monuments that do not allow the collecting of firewood or the building of open campfires at any time. There are other forested areas that are periodically closed to campfires when the fire danger is high. And some forests are just too damp; getting a fire going is more effort than it's worth. Finally, there is the valid ecological argument that continual gathering of firewood at popular campsites results in a denuded forest that is unattractive for future campers. For these reasons you may find it necessary or desirable to carry a lightweight backpacking stove along with enough fuel for your trip. Granted, campfires have a great deal of appeal, but cook stoves are far more efficient when it comes to preparing meals.

If you do build a fire in the forest, safety precautions are a must. Paraphrasing Old Smokey, human carelessness *is* the major cause for forest fires. The most sensible kind of fireplace is one that is dug into the ground. Locate the fire hole in an area that is relatively free of vegetation and overhanging branches. A small rectangle about 12 by 18 inches *dug down to mineral soil* is sufficient. Place any sod from the hole carefully aside. If the soil you remove from the hole is not filled with duff, which is combustible, spread it around the edge of the fire hole to act as a fire break. Otherwise, wet the ground well.

When you get ready to leave the campsite, drown the fire completely and replace all the soil. After the sod has been replaced, the fireplace has disappeared, and the area will soon grow back to its natural state. This would not be the case if you had used rocks to form your fireplace. Smoke-blackened stones, even when strewn about the ground, are a clear sign that someone has camped there before you. And let's face it, we all like to think we were the first people to discover a particularly choice camping spot.

The woods, of course, are not just inhabited by trees. They're also the home of a wide assortment of animals, from mouse size to moose size. In most cases, animals are nothing to worry about. But if you are going into woods that have bears or moose, you should know something about those critters. Moose are so ugly they are beautiful. Mama moose also has a habit of being ornery when she's trying to bring up her kids. So if you do run into a female with calves, give

Downfalls pose one of the problems of hiking in the woods.

them plenty of room to get out of your way. The same is true of bears, be they mothers or others. You might be wise, when going into bear country, to attach a little bell to the bottom of your pack; it will ding as you walk and alert any bruins of your presence. This will help avert a surprise encounter. At night, put all your food in a stuff sack and hang it from the limb of a tree ten to 15 feet off the ground. Don't keep food in your tent, for obvious reasons.

Clearly, animals should be given respect when you are traveling in their forest habitat. However, there's no reason to fear them. As a matter of fact, backpacking in the deep woods is one of the best ways to observe and learn about wildlife ways.

When setting up your tent in the woods, avoid camping under dead trees or trees with dead limbs that might fall on you.

23 Large Trails

Probably the best known of all hiking trails in the country is the Appalachian Trail, extending 2,000 miles from Springer Mountain in Georgia to Mt. Katahdin in Baxter State Park, Maine. The Appalachian Trail is well known to many people throughout the country, but actually there are a great many trails in America which are just as exciting and offer just as much challenge and adventure.

Here's a brief rundown of the "top 25" trails in America.

Resting in the woods along the Appalachian Trail

APPALACHIAN TRAIL

(2,000 miles) From Springer Mountain, Georgia, to Mt. Katahdin, Maine. First proposed in 1921 by Benton McKaye in an article entitled "The Appalachian Trail—An Experiment in Regional Planning," the first mile was blazed just a year later. After that, however, it was considered an impossible task and abandoned. Not until four years later was the project revived by one Arthur Perkins of Hartford, Connecticut, who helped to form the Appalachian Trail Conference. Just 11 years later, the trail was completed. Of all the trails in the East, the Appalachian is the most popular. In some areas it's even overused, with signs of erosion showing. These areas mostly are between points of access closest to large metropolitan areas such as Boston, Washington, New York and Atlanta. In some areas the Appalachian Trail forms the backbone of other trail systems. It is well marked and described in guidebooks, and shelters have been constructed at eight-mile intervals along most of its route. For further information, contact the Appalachian Trail Conference, Inc., P.O. Box 236, Harpers Ferry, WV 25425.

LONG TRAIL

(260 miles) Extending from western Massachusetts to Canada. This trail, developed by the Green Mountain Club and formed in 1910, allows hikers to follow a ridge through forests and over mountain summits without carrying tents or tarp. A total of 70 shelters have been built at about four-mile intervals. The Appalachian Trail overlaps the lower third of Long Trail. Water is plentiful. For detailed information and maps, contact the Green Mountain Club, P.O. Box 889, 43 State St., Montpelier, VT 05602, which produces an excellent guidebook on the Long Trail.

FLORIDA TRAIL

(700 miles) Extending from the Tamiami Trail in the Everglades to Panama City past Lake Okeechobee, through the Ocala National Forest, along the Suwanee River, past Wakulla Springs and through the Appalachicola National Forest. Since much of the trail crosses private land, each hiker must be a member of the Florida Trail Association, but cost of membership is nominal. For information, contact the Florida Trail Association, P.O. Box 13708, Gainesville, FL 32604.

THE OCALA TRAIL

(62 miles) A section of the Florida Trail located on public lands and therefore not requiring membership in the FTA. This trail allows hikers to walk the backbone of Florida over some 30 feet of ancient sands which cover a limestone bed. Under this are many springs and underground streams, while topside are numerous lakes and ponds in a forest of tall pines and oaks. Drinking water is plentiful and camping is allowed anywhere, and excellent fishing is to be found along the way. For detailed maps and information, contact the District Ranger, U.S. Forest Service, Ocala, FL 32670.

PACIFIC CREST TRAIL

(2,400 miles) Extends from Mexican border to Canada. First conceived by Clinton Clarke of Pasadena in 1932, it was only after it became a National Scenic Trail by act of Congress in 1968 that work actually began. Today it is more than two-thirds complete, but one can hike it entirely with certain marked detours, all of them in California. The trail is complete in Washington and Oregon. For further details and maps covering the Washington and Oregon segments, contact the Regional Forester, U.S. Forest Service, P.O. Box 3623, Portland, OR 97208; for California, Regional Forester, U.S. Forest Service, 630 Sansome St., San Francisco, CA 94111.

JOHN MUIR TRAIL

(178 miles) Extends from Yosemite National Park across the Alps of America to the headwaters of the Kings River in California. The John Muir is merely a section of the Pacific Crest Trail, but it leads across an amazing number of high peaks of the Sierra Nevada Range, 94 of them over 13,000 feet and 11 towering more than 14,000 feet. For information contact the Sierra Club, 530 Bush St., San Francisco, CA 94108.

SIERRA CREST TRAIL

(137 miles) Also a segment of the Pacific Crest Trail extending from Mt. Whitney to Tehachapi Pass through primitive wilderness country. Best source of information on this one is the Sierra Club, too.

A high spot along the Appalachian Trail

DESERT CREST TRAIL

The southernmost segment of the Pacific Crest Trail, extends from Tehachapi Pass through the Mohave Desert, through the Angeles and Cleveland National Forests as well as the Coahuila Indian Reservation to a point two miles south of Campo, California, on the Mexican border. Much of this is desert country with summer temperatures in the shade ranging well over 120°. Plan accordingly. Again, consult the Sierra Club for further information on this trail.

CANADIAN RIVER TRAIL, NEW MEXICO

(130 miles) Extending from Ute Lake to Springer and the old Santa Fe Trail. This trail begins in Ute Lake State Park and continues along the Canadian River through Conchas Lake State Park and past Canadian River Canyon. For further information in this and the next two trails listed here, contact the Tourist Division, Dept. of Development, 113 Washington Ave., Santa Fe, NM 87501.

RIO GRANDE TRAIL

(175 miles) Extending from the Colorado border along the Rio Grande River to Belen south of Albuquerque, New Mexico. Much of this lies within the boundaries of the Carson and Santa Fe National Forests.

PECO RIVER TRAIL

(100 miles) From Malaga south of Carlsbad, New Mexico, to Roswell along the Pecos River and through Bottomless Lakes.

BARTRAM TRAIL, ALABAMA

(175 miles) Extending generally along the Tombigbee River from the point where it joins the Mobile River north of the city of Mobile along tributaries to Birmingham where it becomes the Pinhoti Trail extending northeastward to a point just south of Chattanooga. The Bartram Trail Commission has expressed hope that Georgia will link this trail with the Appalachian Trail at Springer Mountain at some future date. For further information, contact Alabama Bureau of

Publicity & Information, State Highway Bldg., Montgomery, AL 36104.

TRANS-OZARK TRAIL

(300 miles) Extending generally from the Oklahoma border across the northern part of Arkansas to Salado through portions of the Ozark National Forest. For details, contact R. D. Murray, 2006 Austin Dr., Fayetteville, AR 72701.

ZENITH TRAIL

(Approximately 3,000 miles) Extending from Big Sur on the California coast to Cape Lookout on the Outer Banks of North Carolina. Only 800 miles of this trail is now ready for hiking (that portion which includes Sequoia-Kings Canyon National Parks, Death Valley National Monument, Desert Wildlife Range, Arizona Strip, Zion National Park, Canyonlands region and Glen Canyon National Recreation Area in Utah-Arizona). Contact North America Trail Complex, P.O. Box 1805, Bloomington, IN 47402.

TECUMSEH TRAIL

(3,500 miles) Extending from the Canadian border near Lake of the Woods in western Ontario to Florida where it would connect up with the Florida Trail. Only a 130-mile section of this trail through southern Indiana from the Ohio River to the Morgan-Monroe State Forest has been established. However, plans call for completion within the next few months. That portion which now is established and ready for hiking lies mostly in the Hoosier National Forest and the proposed Nebo Ridge National Wilderness Area, Yellowwood State Forest and Morgan-Monroe State Forest. For information, contact NO-AMTRAC, P.O. Box 805, Bloomington, IN 47401.

CRAWFORD PATH, NEW HAMPSHIRE

(Oldest trail in the nation, in use since 1820) Extends through the White Mountain National Forest, a unique wilderness. For additional information, contact Supervisor, White Mountain National Forest, P.O. Box 638, Laconia, NH 03246.

FINGER LAKES TRAIL, NEW YORK

(350 miles) Linking the Catskills, Allegheny Mountains across the base of the Finger Lakes to Niagara Falls. It then connects with the Bruce Trail in Canada (Niagara Falls to Tobermory on Georgian Bay). Note: This is only about 60 percent complete with another 25 percent under construction. For additional information, contact the Finger Lakes Trail Conference, Inc., 22 Sturbridge Ln., Pittsford, NY 14534.

LAKE PLACID TRAIL, NEW YORK

(133 miles) Runs north-south through the Adirondacks and the Adirondack Wilderness Preserve. Actually there are hundreds of additional miles of connecting trails in the Forest Preserve, and a trail guide is published by the Adirondack Mountain Club. For information, contact the Adirondack Mountain Club, Inc., 172 Ridge St., Glens Falls, NY 12801.

BUCKEYE TRAIL, OHIO

(500 miles) Extending from the Ohio River east of Cincinnati to Lake Erie west of Cleveland. Now approximately 90 percent complete, the trail was first proposed in 1959. Contact Buckeye Trail Assoc., Inc., P.O. Box 8746, Columbus, OH 43215.

BAKER TRAIL, PENNSYLVANIA

(120 miles) Extending north-south through the Laurel Highlands of west central Pennsylvania. Established in 1950, it's administered by the Pittsburgh Council of American Youth Hostels, 6300 Fifth Ave., Pittsburgh, PA 15232.

CROSS MICHIGAN HIKING TRAIL

(210 miles) Winds across the northern part of Michigan's Lower Peninsula from a point between the towns of Empire-Elberta on Lake Michigan to Tawas City on Lake Huron. It traverses dunes and forestlands and offers an excellent opportunity to fish. Contact Michigan Trail Riders, Inc., Chamber of Commerce, Traverse City, MI 49684.

SHAWNEE HIKING TRAIL, ILLINOIS

(120 miles) Traverses the state from east to west across the Shawnee National Forest. Contact Supervisor, Shawnee Forest, Harrisburg, IL.

TONTO TRAIL, GRAND CANYON NATIONAL PARK

(200 miles) Although a number of trails are available in Grand Canyon, this is considered the most challenging and dramatic by many hikers. Contact Superintendent, Grand Canyon National Park, AZ.

CHESAPEAKE & OHIO CANAL TOWPATH

(186 miles) Extending from Cumberland, Maryland, to Washington, DC, past Harpers Ferry and Antietam Battlefield. Contact Potomac Area Council, AYH, 1501-16th St., NW, Washington, DC 20036.

CALIFORNIA RIDING & HIKING TRAIL

(3,000 miles) A leaf-shaped trail complex around the state including the Sierra Nevada Range and the Coast Range with a stem south from Tejon Pass. First organized in 1945, some 750 miles have been completed with a total of 2,500 miles of secured right-of-way. Contact State Office of Tourism, 1400 Tenth St., Sacramento, CA 95814.

24 City Trails

When most city-dwellers think of planning a hike, they think in terms of a two-hour ride by automobile (at the very least) to get out of the city and into the closest wilderness area. But the fact is there are a great number of hiking trails within (or near) many of the largest cities.

And you would be wrong if you were to think that a city-area trail must be overrun with crowds and not worth seeing. A great number of these hiking trails cross some of the finest hiking terrain anywhere, and many of them are surprisingly little known, considering their nearby locations. Of course, a city-area trail may not afford you the same solitary wilderness experience that a trip to the Smokies or the Rockies might, but many of them do offer unique sights.

One example is the Palisades Long Path, which follows along the top of the Palisades, just across the Hudson River from New York City. This trail, which can be reached by walking across the George Washington Bridge from New York, extends north from the bridge to the New York line and beyond. It offers some of the best views of the Hudson River Valley to be found anywhere along the river's length, and is ideal for the beginning hiker.

Other cities have equally enticing hiking areas, many of which make ideal one-day trips.

EMERALD NECKLACE TRAIL

Cleveland, Ohio, extends in a great arc through the city park system which rings the city. Contact Cleveland Metropolitan Park District, 1370 Ontario St., Cleveland, OH 44113.

BLUE HILLS TRAILS

Boston, Massachusetts, south of the city. Contact Boston Parks District, City Building, Boston, MA.

SCIOTO RIVER TRAILS

Columbus, Ohio, extending along the Scioto River. Contact Metropolitan Parks District, Columbus, OH.

NORTH AND SOUTH MOUNTAIN PARK TRAILS

Phoenix, Arizona, encompassing 15 miles. Contact Park & Recreation Dept., Phoenix, AZ.

EAST BAY SKYLINE TRAIL

San Francisco Bay Area (14 miles). Contact East Bay Regional Park District, San Francisco, CA.

PENITENCIA CREEK TRAIL

San Jose, California (5.5 miles). Contact Parks & Recreation Dept., San Jose, CA.

HIGHLINE CANAL TRAIL

Denver (18 miles). Contact South Suburban Metropolitan Recreation & Park District, Denver, CO.

FORT CIRCLE PARKS TRAIL

Washington, DC (7.9 miles). Contact National Park Service, Capitol Parks Division, Washington, DC.

STONE MOUNTAIN TRAIL

Atlanta (6.51 miles). Contact Stone Mountain Memorial Assoc., Atlanta, GA.

ILLINOIS PRAIRIE PATH

Chicago (22.7 miles). Contact Parks & Recreation, City Building, Chicago, IL.

BELLE ISLE HIKING TRAIL

Detroit (.9 miles). Contact City of Detroit Parks & Recreation Dept., Detroit, MI.

PALISADES LONG PATH

Palisades Interstate Park, New York City (11 miles). Contact Palisades Interstate Park Comm., New York, NY.

HARRIMAN LONG PATH

Harriman State Park, New York City (16 miles). Contact Palisades Interstate Park Comm., New York, NY.

FAIRMOUNT PARK TRAIL

Philadelphia (8.5 miles). Contact Fairmount Park Commission, Philadelphia, PA.

LAKE WASHINGTON PATH

Seattle (2.5 miles). Contact Dept. of Parks & Recreation, Seattle, WA.

LAKE PARK TRAIL

(3.1 miles) and

WARNIMOUNT PARK TRAIL
(1.5 miles), Milwaukee. Contact Milwaukee County Parks Comm., Milwaukee, WI.

With the enactment of the National Trails System Act of 1968 and with added emphasis being placed upon hiking by government recreation agencies at all levels, the future for this most worthwhile leisure activity is indeed bright. "We foresee a network of trails interlacing across the nation," said a spokesman for the Bureau of Outdoor Recreation in Washington, "so that one day those desiring to hike can actually travel across America in any direction from border to border." That day may not be many years away.

Appendix

MAJOR MANUFACTURERS OF
BACKPACKING EQUIPMENT AND RELATED GEAR

Most companies will send you their free catalogs on request; several will have no printed material available; to some, you will have to pay a nominal fee for information; a few will ignore your entreaties altogether.

ADVENTURE 16
4620 Alvarado Cyn Rd.
San Diego, CA 92120

AIR LIFT
2217 Roosevelt Ave.
Berkeley, CA 94703

ALPENLITE
3891 N. Ventura Ave.
Ventura, CA 93001

ALPINE DESIGNS
316 S. Lexington
Cheyenne, WY 82001

ALTRA
5541 Central Ave.
Boulder, CO 80301

L.L. BEAN, INC.
Freeport, ME 04033

BLACK ICE
2310 Laurel #4
Napa, CA 94559

BROWNING
Route 1
Morgan, UT 84050

BUCCANEER MFG.
35 York St.
Brooklyn, NY 11201

CAMEL MFG. CO.
P.O. Box 835
Knoxville, TN 37901

CAMP 7 INC.
802 S. Sherman
Longmont, CO 80501

CAMP-WAYS INC.
P.O. Box 61157
Los Angeles, CA 90061

CANNONDALE
9 Brookside Place
Georgetown, CT 06829

CASE & SONS
  CUTLERY
20 Russell Blvd.
Bradford, PA 16701

CENTURY PRIMUS
1462 U.S. Route #20
P.O. Box 188
Cherry Valley, IL 61016

CLASS-5 INC.
1480 66th St.
Emeryville, CA 94608

COGHLANS LTD.
121 Irene St.
Winnipeg MB Canada

COLEMAN CO. INC.
250 N. St. Francis
Wichita, KS 67201

DANNER SHOE MFG.
Box 22204
Portland, OR 97222

DEXTER SHOE CO.
31 St. James Ave.
Boston, MA 02116

DONNER MOUNTAIN
  CORP.
2110 Fifth St.
Berkeley, CA 94710

DUNHAM
Vernon Dr.
P.O. Box 813
Brattleboro, VT 05301

DUOFOLD INC.
Mohawk, NY 13407

ESTWING MFG. CO.
2647 8th St.
Rockford, IL 61101

FABIANO SHOE CO.
850 Summer St.
S. Boston, MA 02127

FAMOUS TRAILS
3602 Kurtz
San Diego, CA 92110

FORREST
  MOUNTAINEERING
1517 Platte St.
Denver, CO 80202

GEE CORP.
323 Geary St.
San Francisco, CA 94102

W.L. GORE & ASSOC.
2401 Singerly Rd.
P.O. Box 1220
Elkton, MD 21921

GUTMANN CUTLERY
900 S. Columbus
Mt. Vernon, NY 10550

HENDERSON CAMP
  PROD.
300 W. Washington St.
Chicago, IL 60606

HIMALAYAN
INDUSTRIES
301 Mulberry
Pine Bluff, AR 71601

HIRSCH WEIS
380 SE Spokane St.
Portland, OR 97202

HOBSON CO.
P.O. Box 2312
La Puente, CA 91746

JAN SPORT CO.
Paine Field Industrial
Park
Everett, WA 98204

JOHNSON CAMPING
INC.
P.O. Box 966
Binghamton, NY 13902

KELTY PACK INC.
9281 Borden Ave.
Sun Valley, CA 91352

LOWE ALPINE
SYSTEMS
P.O. Box 189
Lafayette, CO 80026

MOSS TENT WORKS
P.O. Box 309
Camden, ME 04843

MOUNTAIN
EQUIPMENT INC.
1636 S. Second St.
Fresno, CA 93702

MOUNTAIN SAFETY
RESEARCH
P.O. Box 3978
Terminal Station
Seattle, WA 98124

NORTH FACE
1234 Fifth St.
Berkeley, CA 94710

OPTIMUS INC.
P.O. Box 1950
Bridgeport, CT 06601

OREGON FREEZE
DRY FOODS INC.
P.O. Box 1048
Albany, OR 97321

OUTDOOR VENTURE
CORP.
Highway 92
Stearns, KY 42647

QP PANTS
3300 Atlantic Blvd.
Jacksonville, FL 32207

QUABAUG RUBBER
CO.
17 School St.
N. Brookfield, MA 01535

RAICHLE MOLITOR
USA
Geneva Rd.
Brewster, NY 10509

RAVEN IND. INC.
205 E. 6th St.
Box 1007
Sioux Falls, SD 57101

RED WING SHOE CO.
Red Wing, MN 55066

RELIANCE
PRODUCTS
1830 Dublin Ave.
Winnipeg Canada Mb

RICH-MOOR CORP.
P.O. Box 2728
Van Nuys, CA 91404

HANK ROBERTS INC.
410 Sunset
Suite 100
Longmont, CO 80501

ROYAL ROBBINS INC.
Box 4536
Modesto, CA 95352

SCHRECK
WHOLESALE INC.
3100 N. Lincoln Ave.
Chicago, IL 60657

SIERRA DESIGNS
247 Fourth St.
Oakland, CA 94607

SIERRA WEST
6 E. Yanonall St.
Santa Barbara, CA 93101

SLUMBERJACK INC.
2103 Humboldt St.
Los Angeles, CA 90031

PETER STORM INC.
15115 NE 90th
Redmond, WA 98052

SUMMIT PRODUCTS
INC.
43 Park Lane
Brisbane, CA 94005

SUNSHINE LEISURE
20310 Plummer St.
Chatsworth, CA 91311

TEXSPORT
P.O. Box 55326
Houston, TX 77255

3M THERMAL
INSULATION
PRODUCTS
3M Center
St. Paul, MN 55144

T P MFG.
12752 Monarch St.
Garden Grove, CA 92641

TRAILWISE MFG.
221 West 1st St.
Kewanee, IL 61443

VASQUE
419 Bush St.
Red Wing, MN 55066

WALKER SHOE CO.
P.O. Drawer 1167
Asheboro, NC 27203

WENZEL CO.
1280 Research Blvd.
St. Louis, MO 63132

WHITE STAG MFG. CO.
5100 SE Harney Dr.
Portland, OR 97206

WIGWAM MILLS INC.
3402 Crocker Ave.
Sheboygan, WI 53081

WILDERNESS EXPERIENCE
20675 Nordhoff St.
Chatsworth, CA 91311

WOOLRICH INC.
Mill St.
Woolrich, PA 17779

CARL ZEISS INC.
1 Zeiss Dr.
Thornwood, NY 10594